Armenian Proverbs and Expressions

Armenian Proverbs and Expressions

A Collection from
the Early Detroit Armenian Community
in Delray and Elsewhere

Collected and Edited by
Susan Kadian Gopigian

Illustrations by
Susan Collier Bolt

Shoushan Books
Bloomfield Hills, Michigan
2019

Published by Shoushan Books, Bloomfield Hills, MI 48301

Manufactured in the United States of America

23 22 21 20 19 5 4 3 2 1

ISBN 978-0-9801453-3-5

Book Publishing Consultants, Alice Nigoghosian, Dearborn, MI
Manuscript editing by Wendy Warren Keebler, Beverly Hills, MI
Graphic design and typesetting by Cathy Jacobs Brito, Ann Arbor, MI
All photographs by Garon Gopigian unless otherwise indicated or those prior to 1999. Photos prior to 1999 courtesy various family members.
Printed by McNaughton & Gunn, Saline, MI
Binding by Dekker Bookbinding, Grand Rapids, MI

The paper used in this publication meets the minimum requirements of the American National Standard for Information Sciences–Permanence of paper for Printed Library Materials, ANSI z39.48-1984.

Note to the Reader:

Given the existence of several transliteration systems for the Armenian language, the spelling of place names and some words varies widely among scholars and in the reference literature. Sometimes Armenian phrases may reflect local dialects and pronunciations.

Dedicated to all the silenced voices

Of the 1915 Armenian Genocide,

And the Armenian survivors and immigrants

Who lived to tell their stories

And kept oral tradition alive

For their posterity. Lest we forget.

❖

"It's a debt that we,

the living, owe to the dead;

if we forget,

it will be as if they died again."

—Simon Wiesenthal

Epigram

Oh, ye souls, whose bones nature has altered... and
ground into the earth.
The shards glistening
in the Der el Zor Desert...
Whose tears nourished
the soil and dried.
Your wails arise as the sun stokes the hot sand.
The steam evaporates,
and no one hears your cries.

Susan Kadian Gopigian

Epigram Meaning: An Inscription

The victims of the 1915 Armenian Genocide have been buried in many years of desert sand. I'm haunted by the experiences of my family members who lived through this and those who perished. We, the children and grandchildren, are their voices. Often my thoughts go back to their plight, and I journey vicariously with my ancestors as they were exiled from their Turkish towns and villages into the Der el Zor Desert. It is as if their soundless voices rise up to remind me never to forget. Somehow their repressed pain is transmitted by some spiritual bond that cannot be seen or heard . . . yet vibrates to the soul, forming an unresolved knot that needs to be released. Surely, their deaths need recognition, or they will have died in vain.

How can this be? It's unexplainable how their deaths still impact our lives! Sometimes I envision my great-grandfather on horseback, ordered to doctor wounded Turkish soldiers in the War of 1895. It was his last stand; he was felled by a Turkish bullet, as Uncle Krikor Doctorian recalled.

Even today, remembering the story of my mother-in-law Dzaghig Gopigian's time in the Der el Zor Desert causes me to shudder. No human being should have to bury her four-year-old son, clawing the earth to protect his body from vultures after he was butted by a Turk's gun. She lived to tell her story.

Sometimes I'm on Rock Pert in Shabinkraissar, transported back to my father's extended family (*kertasdan*) of thirty-five to forty members, where thousands of heroic Armenian villagers sought shelter from Turkish invaders. Courageously, 250 Armenian men and boys waged a lopsided war of survival against a formidable army of Turkish soldiers. The Armenians were overwhelmed.

After twenty-eight heroic days on the summit, only forty-seven survived,[1] including my eleven-year-old uncle, Charlie (Garabed). He ran down the mount to escape. They won the battle on bravery but lost the war on Rock Pert. My Armenian-French cousin Mathios Sormayan narrated the experience on tape as recounted to him by his Shabinkraissar countrymen.

Thankfully, the immigrants and survivors perpetuated the tradition of oral history

1 Aram Haigaz, *The Fall of the Erie* (Boston: Ararat, 1935), p. 179.

and kept this poignant period of the 1915 Armenian Genocide alive and to be remembered… lest we forget.

❖

Shortly after writing this section, I came across an August 2012 article in the *New York Times* titled "In Andalusia, on the Trail of Inherited Memories." Fortuitously, it opened up and confirmed the existence of a world of an unconscious sense of identity linking the past to the present. French psychologist Anne Ancelin Schutzenberger offers a succinct explanation of the concept of repressed pain transmitted across generations. This information adds credence to my consciousness of the pain of ancestral victims of the Armenian Genocide. She writes that "we are links in a chain of generations, unconsciously affected by their suffering or unfinished business until we acknowledge the past."[2] Schutzenberger calls this the "ancestor syndrome," which confirms the rather strange phenomenon of unconscious generational pain. Aline Ohanesian labels this "trans-generational grief."[3] There it is! A validated explanation that past pain doesn't cease with time but only when resolved.

---

2 Quoted in Doreen Carvajal, "In Andalusia, on the Trail of Inherited Memories," *New York Times*, August 21, 2012, p. D3.

3 Aline Ohanesian, *Orhan's Inheritance* (Chapel Hill: Algonquin, 2015), p. 310.

Contents

Preface

"To forget our ancestors is to be a brook without a source, a tree without a root."
– Chinese proverb

It has taken many decades of recording to organize and create this collection of Armenian proverbs. At times, it was a daunting task and a challenge, as my Armenian-language skills were limited. Always the motivating force has been my love of Armenian lore, listening to old-country stories, and the enchantment of the language. This all started in my childhood home, where the Armenian language was the required means of communication by my father. Although he immigrated before the 1915 Armenian Genocide without English-language skills, he learned to speak and write English fluently and read three newspapers daily: the *Detroit Free Press*, the *Detroit News*, and the *Detroit Times*. His sage advice was: "You will always learn English, but you must master Armenian at home." His fear was that we would become Americanized and lose our Armenian identity. His adamant reminder: "I lost my whole family *(kertasdan)* in the 1915 Genocide so you could keep your Armenian heritage."

On the other hand, my mother's world was reading Armenian books. This was her pleasure. As a child, I often trudged in rain, cold, or snow to check out another unread book for her from the Campbell Branch Library on Fort Street, which had an Armenian-language section. We had a system: books read were marked with a lightly penciled N (my mother's initial) on the right-hand corner of the first blank page. On quiet evenings, she would retell the stories in Armenian, especially if there was a moral lesson to be taught. I learned about Victor Hugo at an early age, before I took any high school literature classes. Those treks to the library paid off with wonderful adventures into the world of books. This was where my love of listening to and reading stories began.

It's important to note that my mother never mastered the English language. She spoke broken English and read English abysmally. When she read a word like *magician*, she would think it referred to an Armenian, as most Armenian surnames end in *-ian*. Furthermore, when my brother George showed her his report card, with checks in the social behavior column, she didn't understand the marks or the English meaning and naively believed it was a good report. I told her, "He talks too much in class."

Conveniently, my father's admonishment worked. Armenian became the household language, and my mother's world remained undisturbed and continued to be comfortably Armenian.

What I didn't realize then, and appreciate now, is the great advantage it afforded me later as I collected Armenian proverbs and folktales. Besides speaking the language, my mother taught us to read and write elementary Armenian, which was an added benefit to recording Armenian proverbs and stories from the old country. Playing outside after school may have been an inviting option, but it was not to be. Learning a very foreign Armenian alphabet became our after-school task. At the time, it seemed unfair, but my mother's wisdom prevailed in her encouraging words (in Armenian, of course): "Whatsoever you learn is a golden bracelet on your arm, to be used when needed." It was, and learning to read and write Armenian became an asset.

This description of my background wouldn't be complete without mentioning Delray. My two brothers and I were born in this special, obscure corner of southwest Detroit, Michigan, where my parents settled. This collection of proverbs all began in Delray with the immigration of Armenians from Turkish Armenia after the 1915 Armenian Genocide. In the early decades of the twentieth century, Delray was a vital, bustling haven for émigrés. It was a conglomeration of Hungarians, Italians, Poles, Armenians, and others. Delray was a paradigm of immigrant communities across America, a "Little Europe." Like other settlements, Delray had a unique structure of "clustering" with similar folk, making it a comfortable, stratified community, with different nationalities functioning side by side, diverse yet alike in creating a new homeland. And so it was in our small, esoteric Armenian enclave; everything was conveniently Armenian. Everyone spoke Armenian, though with different village dialects, exposing us to old-country stories, anecdotes, proverbs, human-interest tales of the antics of Delray folk, and less pronounced memories of the Armenian Genocide (which were quietly whispered away from children). I always listened with eager, curious ears and mentally recorded them. These stories captured and ignited my imagination, transporting me to a past world.

For the Armenian immigrants, remembering life as it once was and sharing their stories helped bridge the vast void between their homeland and their new adopted country. Somehow this transitional communication succeeded in bonding the varied Armenian peoples in Delray. We were truly enriched by the purveyors of these magical tales, which enabled me to preserve what I had heard. The immigrants and survivors were the preservationists of our Armenian oral tradition.

One morning, I awoke with an onerous and startling question: "Who is going to know about this epochal time in Delray after the Armenian immigration, unless this period is recorded?" Certainly, it would take discerning wisdom, foresight, and academic savvy to grasp the significance of this era, especially the implications for the survivors and their children. In fact, this would require much academic research. Fearing that this period would be lost, I thought I could at least contribute a glimpse into this world, as I perceived it, through the eyes of a youngster and from the perspective of how it influenced my life. My love of Armenian folklore stems from my exposure to these immigrants. Armenian oral history is the thread that binds the survivors of the Armenian Genocide to my generation, giving us an insight into their past. I am indebted to these brave souls.

Now time is speeding by, taking memories into its fold and my generation with it. We, the first generation born of immigrant parents, are the last vestige of our residual Armenian culture. As folklorist Susie Hoogasian Villa wrote, "If this ethnic lore is to be recorded and preserved for future study, it must be collected before the Americanization process becomes complete."[1] Although I collected as much as I could, I wish I had listened more and recorded even more diligently. If only the clock could magically be turned back to the 1930s through the 1980s, when the immigrant generation was still with us. Somehow our generation didn't take time to listen. Our ears were deafened to their untold stories. We were too focused on assimilating. We wanted to be American. Now it's an uncaptured past. It was so available in those early years of acclimation, yet regrettably, there was not an awareness of the importance of Armenian oral history. We were living history and didn't know it. With hindsight, I realize more and more the significance of this bygone period and feel compelled to preserve my experience rooted in Delray. The impetus to collect is credited to my friend Susie Hoogasian Villa, who reminded me, "Time is running out, so start collecting Armenian folklore." She was my mentor and persistent motivator to record when it was not a popular pursuit. This collection of Armenian proverbs is my humble effort to preserve some semblance of Armenian oral history, as I heard and recorded it, and it focuses on the influence of the Delray community and its significance for collecting folklore and proverbs.

---

1 Susie Hoogasian Villa, *100 Armenian Tales* (Detroit: Wayne State University Press, 1966), pp. 22–23.

Acknowledgments

"Man with man."
– Armenian proverb

"No man is an island, entire of itself," proclaimed the seventeenth-century English poet John Donne. A similar philosophy was expressed more simply in the Armenian adage *mart, martov* ("man with man"). As both indicate, progress is never the result of one person's endeavor; it is a process that involves the input of others. Many individuals helped bring this Armenian proverb collection to fruition as it started with a seed and blossomed into a recognizable entity; encouragement, direction, and advice came from my family, friends, and professionals.

The seed for collecting Armenian proverbs was planted in my childhood. Being Armenian was very important to my father, and knowing the Armenian language was important to my mother. She used Armenian proverbs and folklore in our home. Not only were my parents the seminal reason and motivation for my interest in collecting, but they actually prepared the fertile ground for this endeavor.

In the 1960s, Susie Hoogasian Villa urged me to record Armenian oral history—proverbs, folktales, folk medicine, and anecdotes. Susie's reminder was "Time is running out, and soon our parents' generation will be gone and with them all oral tradition." She was a tough, unrelenting taskmaster. Often I accompanied her to folklore seminars, always encouraged with "Are you working on your collection? Keep at it!" Her constant prodding and questioning kept me on a focused track.

Someone Susie felt was invaluable was my publishing consultant, Alice Nigoghosian. "Don't lose touch with her," Susie urged. Much credit is due to Alice for her persistent, periodic reminders to complete the Armenian collection.

Sometimes chiding and help from family members bring resolve. For many years, my youngest son, Brion, would ridicule me about completing the collection by claiming, "You've been collecting proverbs since I was born." Meanwhile, my middle son, Garon, encouraged me with his assistance to record and computerize the proverb collection. At times, revisions numbering beyond patience, he was not only encouraging but kept me on a focused track with determination and resolve. Finally, my eldest son, Christopher, contributed by collecting historical Delray data.

Acknowledgments

I am grateful to retired University of Detroit professor Dr. James Callow, who was instrumental in structuring the proverb format for easy computer access. My deep appreciation also goes to Lucy Ardash, Teryl Minasian Asher, Elena Calvillo, Araxie Choukourian, Mae Derdarian, Nancy Kezlarian Herrick, Mark Kadian, Barbara Megerian, and Jane Ferguson Mooradian for editorial suggestions and advice; to Marian Engoian Fontichiaro, Simon Javizian, and Margaret Lehoczky Kocsisko for Delray confirmation data; to Audrey Mooradian for research material; and to Sylvie Merian for expertise and guidance in creating the colophon, which added an ancient format. Special gratitude goes to Sebouh Avedikian and Anahit and Dickran Toumajan for their academic Armenian translation and transliteration of the proverbs, and my heartfelt appreciation is due to the late Hourig Jacobs, who spent numerous hours using her Armenian expertise in translating, transliterating, editing, and reentering additions to the book. This book would have been impossible without her devoted assistance. It helped that she found joy, and at times amazement, in the many proverbs she had never heard even in her native Beirut.

I am grateful to Wendy Warren Keebler for her expertise as an English-language editor—efficient, punctual, and discerning. In the artistic venue, which visually enriches the book, I'm grateful to Cathy Jacobs Brito for her invaluable creativity in graphic design and her proficiency in the Armenian language. Finally, the imaginative pen-and-ink etchings that enhanced the proverb topics and the beautifully imaged cover design are by my friend and endearing artist Susan Collier Bolt. Susan's creative artistry brings visual wonder to the book.

I could not have completed the proverb collection without the help of these people, *mart, martov* ("man with man"). I'm truly grateful.

Susan Kadian Gopigian

Prologue 1

THE DELRAY COMMUNITY

"A tree stands taller when it knows its roots."
– Armenian proverb

The purpose of this first prologue is to capture the bygone period of immigration history that gives context to my collection of Armenian proverbs. It is very important to know where we came from as children of immigrants and the area that embraced us.

Delray! Who remembers this immigrant settlement in southwest Detroit, Michigan, a rich amalgam of varied ethnic cultures? Memory has restorative power and can awaken the past and make it live again. Now the Delray[1] I knew as a child is gone, but it was real, and I lived it. Today those early years seem like a hiccup in time, a pause that disappeared with the immigrants, never to be captured again, only to be swallowed up in history. Those early childhood memories of the 1930s and 1940s are still banked in the recesses of my mind, to be recalled for reminiscences with family and friends. Some are heartwarming, some are sadly nostalgic, some are whimsical, and some are folkloric, but all are memorable and meaningful.

The indomitable immigrant spirit that prevailed in the early twentieth century is gone. The cacophony of foreign voices along the streets no longer fills the air. The once busy shops are abandoned, shuttered, or razed, some with crumbling graffiti-covered walls. The schools that educated thousands of boisterous children lie in vacated hollows. In the midst of weed-covered fields stand a few forlorn houses, but on some streets, well-kept homes remind one of the past. Only the church spires give witness to the fortitude and spiritual strength of what was once a vibrant community. The era of this historical immigration settlement has passed, and now time has vaporized it into oblivion. Today the Delray streets are barren of people and activity.

---

1 According to Wikipedia, Delray's name was adopted and approved November 11, 1905, and it was annexed to Detroit. Located on the southwest side of Detroit, it extends south to River Rouge, east to the Detroit River, west to Fort Street and I-75, north to Dragoon at Fort Wayne, and farther north to Clark Street.

What exists is a small community struggling for survival. Delray homes are being torn down to make way for a new international bridge.[2]

In the early twentieth century, Delray was abloom with hope and gratitude, and bustling and bursting with energy.[3] For the newly arrived immigrants, America was the destination for a new lease on life. The Statue of Liberty may have extended her welcoming torch to the homeless émigrés, but Delray gave them a second homeland and a safe shelter, especially for the exiled Armenians after the 1915 Genocide. It is believed that the first Armenian immigrant in Michigan settled in Delray. The first Armenian Apostolic Church service was held in a church at Erie and Anderson Streets in Delray in 1908.[4]

Besides being separated from departed loved ones, their familial homeland, and their traditional means of earning a living, the immigrants had to adapt to a completely foreign environment. Settling in America presented many great problems of adjustment for them; how to adapt was a challenge. It was both a difficult time and a time of naivety, as the immigrants were encumbered with lack of language skills, shelter, employment, and finances. These were problematic societal hurdles, but the spirit of gratitude and hope always prevailed and encouraged the immigrants. The opportunity of freedom in America inspired their souls to succeed. Anything after their devastating past was an upward swing toward a better life and a new beginning. This freedom from oppression was a huge gift for the Delray Armenians.

The 1920s through the 1940s could be considered the years of settlement and acclimation in Delray. Slowly, the reality of earning a living set in. Jobs, jobs, jobs: jobs to send money back to scattered family members, jobs to feed the family, and jobs to establish a home. Economics was a driving force for survival, and Delray was a magnet for employment. The good news spread: Detroit was the city of opportunity for work! Ford Motor Company, Ternstedt, Solvay Process Company, Michigan Malleable Iron, Michigan Brass, and others were encouraging sources of needed jobs within walking distance or easily accessible by trolley car. I often

---

2 In 2010, the Delray site was being considered for the Detroit International Crossing, which would lead to the demolition of the vast majority of the Delray neighborhood. Currently, this plan is in process.

3 In 1930, Delray had approximately 23,000 residents; as of the 2010 Census, the area had a population of only 2,763.

4 Dr. Ashod Rhaffi Aprahamian, *Remarkable Rebirth: The Early History of Armenians in Detroit* (Detroit: Elizabeth Aprahamian, 1957), p. 44.

wondered how the men managed to get to work. My childhood friend Justina said her father walked from Harrington to Crossley to work at Solvay Process Company, a mere four blocks or so.

It was around 1939, I remember, when an upsurge of high school graduates started working at the Ford Motor Company's Rouge plant, enabling them to purchase a basic Ford model. With employment on the upswing, drivers of these cars began to preen on the Delray streets. These new graduates often supported their families during the Depression years. This growth in jobs was seen across all ethnic groups within the Delray community. But how did these varied groups cope inside Delray?

With the influx of Armenians, Hungarians, Italians, Poles, Slovakians, Germans, and others, the necessity to survive in the New World required wisdom, resourcefulness, and hopeful dreams. Not only was Delray a self-contained community, but the diverse immigrants formed a functioning, comfortable solution by clustering with similar folk to support their respective ethnicities. This need for familiarity was a stepping stone toward acclimation. And so it happened that Delray became the new "Old Country" and functioned as a somewhat insular community. This small enclave of different nationalities in southwest Detroit developed into a harmonious mosaic of ethnic cultures, living side by side, alike yet different, living in a new homeland in a new world, while holding on to their native cultures. They formed a secure, comfortable, and functioning environment.

West Jefferson Avenue was the hub of Delray, the heartbeat and drumroll of activity. Along this main shopping thoroughfare, the cadence of foreign accents filled the air, with a mixture of Hungarian, Armenian, Polish, and other ethnic voices. Neighbors and friends exchanging gossip, family happenings, and news events continued the socialization process from home to public shopping. In short, shopping was not only for necessities but became an affordable social event.

These ethnic groups were stratified. Polish people surrounded the south end of Dearborn Street with their beautiful twin-spired St. John Cantius Church, built in 1923, which still stands. Following eastward, many Christian and Jewish Hungarians settled around West End Street. Since the Hungarian population was extensive, it established many needed shops; even the signs up and down West Jefferson had posted on the doors *Magyar Uzlet* (Hungarian Shop). It is said that the Delray Hungarian community was the largest Hungarian population outside of Budapest, with more than fifty small businesses serving its needs. It was known as "Hunky Town."

Positively impacting this community on the Jefferson strip were such shops as Lehoczky's Fancy Pastry Shop, renowned for its delicious Hungarian walnut torte and bishop's bread. This special torte, filled with walnuts and layers of buttercream frosting, was unusually delicious. It was the ultimate desired wedding cake for all Delray brides. Many of us were privileged to have Lehoczky's bake our wedding cakes. This specialty pastry shop, which opened in 1934, served many high-end restaurants in metropolitan Detroit. The delicious buttery scent of the pastries, along with the old-time atmosphere, gave it a European aura. It was one of the last shops to leave Delray, in the early 1970s, reopening as the Fancy Pastry Shop in Allen Park.

My favorite shop was Zuieback's. It was a fashionable women's clothing store unsurpassed by any other in the area. Who could ever believe there would be such a stylish shop in this ethnic community of Delray? The window displays were a sight to behold, a visual pleasure. Window shopping was a way to fantasize about things that were unaffordable. My friend Marian said she would walk to Jefferson just to gaze at a pair of white tasseled boots that she couldn't afford to buy but loved to look at. There was much of this delusional joy in just looking. After all, these were the Depression years. The first time I ever saw a woven leather shoe from Mexico was in Zuieback's window. The shoe was called a *huarache* and became much in demand. Zuieback's brings me a leap of joy when I remember the beautiful burnt-orange leopard-collared coat with six front pleats that my mother purchased for me. It cost about seven dollars, a huge amount for the hard Depression years. To this day, I remember how I loved that coat—even now, it would be retro-chic.

Another much-trafficked store in the business area was Neisner Bros., Inc. 5 cent to $1.00 at the corner of West Jefferson and Dearborn. If ever there was a magical meeting place, it was Neisner, with its many departments. It was a magnet for shopping, and we called it the "dime store." The moment one entered the double doors, the wafting aroma of delicious steamed hot dogs was intoxicating. What a special treat! This was the closest experience to eating out, which was nonexistent in those Depression days. So this sometime pleasure, in a cozy warm bun with a mug of frothy root beer from the tap, was heavenly and a welcomed change from traditional ethnic food. At the entrance, opposite the hot-dog counter, was the music section with the *Your Hit Parade* song sheets. It was a thrill to hear the Saturday *Your Hit Parade* songs on the radio and then buy the song sheets at Neisner. Jeanette MacDonald and Nelson Eddy were often imitated in song at our home. This magical dime store had everything: candy, jewelry, towels, keys to be made, picture frames, you name it. Neisner employed many young Delray women. It was exciting to see your Delray friends working as salespeople.

Behind Neisner Bros., on Dearborn Street, was a reputable Jewish poultry-processing business. It was a magnet for the Delray community. Since the people were fussy about the quality of chickens for cooking, this business served their needs and thrived. Saturdays were the busiest, and comments could be heard as they sized up the chickens, like "That chicken is old," "That chicken is too thin," "That chicken looks sickly, and you can't make soup with it," and on and on. It was an assembly line; you picked the chicken, and they slaughtered it. I often accompanied my mother and watched this unpleasant procedure, then went home to pluck the feathers.

Considering the hardship of the Depression years, it is difficult to understand how this small community supported so many stores. Besides the shops mentioned above, there were Gardner-White, Henig's, Kohlenberg Furniture Company, Swatlow's, Leightman's, Lockeman's Hardware, Pupko's, and Zolkower's, to name a few. Despite the times, these shops were patronized by many immigrants. Although they were thrifty by nature, they seemed to have money for special family needs and special occasions and kept the retail market busy. The niece of the Swatlow's Department Store owners said they had a large Polish clientele for communion, confirmation, special event, and Sunday attire.

Most of the retailers were Hungarian Jewish immigrants, and their beautifully displayed and amply supplied shops made West Jefferson a dynamic retail center. They enhanced our West Jefferson shopping and appealed to the many needs of this multi-ethnic community.

With the growth of the local Jewish population, a synagogue was established in 1915 on West Jefferson, above a bank. "Ten years later [1925], they built a synagogue on Burdeno Street . . . for their First Hebrew Congregation of Delray known also as the Orthodox Hungarian Jewish Congregation. It was Detroit's first Orthodox synagogue west of Woodward."[5] Now that building is used as a church.

Amid the Delray shops, standing next to each other, were the Grande and Hungarian Delray theaters. They were the greatest source of entertainment during the gloomy days of the Depression and lifted the optimism of the people.

---

5 *Jewish News*, September 25–October 1, 2014, p. 26.

Across from the theaters, it is worth mentioning the impressive, iconic Peninsular Bank and Delray Post Office building on West Jefferson. Also on West Jefferson is a beautiful limestone bank building notable for its art deco simplicity. All of these buildings were frequented by the Delray immigrants. Farther east on West Jefferson is the still-functioning Delray Fire Station Number 29 with bright red doors, and on the corner of Crossley was Vartian's Drug Store and Cantor's Men's Store. Down the street, on the opposite side, was Delray General Hospital, built in 1904 and closed in 1991.

At South and Yale Streets looms the majestic Holy Cross Church, serving the Hungarian Catholics, while the Protestants attended the Hungarian Reformed Church at Vanderbilt and West End Streets. Nearby was another Hungarian temple on Dearborn Street, the Gor Kath Magyar Templom. To the south of West End Street, near the Detroit River, was another enclave of Hungarians called the Magyar Tziganes (Hungarian Gypsies). They were a colorful part of the Delray scene and added a bounce to the dismal Depression years of the 1930s, with their costumes, boisterous children, fortune-tellers, and musicians. On weekends, West Jefferson became a stage for entertainment. I remember even my mother and aunt being enticed, timidly, into the strange adventure of having their fortunes told in a folding tent. On the street, it was uplifting and soothing to hear the melodious and passionate violin strains filter through the air. The Delray Tziganes brought an atmosphere of musical fluidity with their violins, their hearts were strings for emotion, and their faces emoted the love of music. Their musical performances were enjoyed at Delray clubs, notably the Hungarian Village Night Club. Even east-siders traveled to Delray for entertainment. My friend Barbara remembers that her parents were Saturday-night attendees for great Hungarian food and beautiful violin music. Other gathering places were Al's Bar, Joey's Stable, Hungarian Kitchen, and Twin Six Club. Delray was jumping with activity for young adults at the many clubs.

My mother was so impressed with the Gypsy violinists that she hired one of the musicians, a stern, stately gentleman, to teach my brother George to play. She purchased a violin, on a monthly payment plan, from J. L. Hudson's Department Store. Again, it was a financial stretch for those times. On lesson days, my mother's good intentions were often hampered by the disappearance of my brother, leaving me desperately searching for him. He feared the demanding teacher's discipline, but the strict training paid off, and he became first violinist at Southwestern High School.

The children of Hungarians and the Hungarian Tziganes, as well as others, attended the James McMillan School on West End Street. It was the dominant elementary school in Delray. Built in 1894, it was the oldest Detroit public school, serving kindergarten through eighth grade, until its closure in 1999. The building has since been razed.

Moving east from West End Street, the Armenian refugees settled side by side on many blocks between Crossley, Solvay, Cottrell, Green, Harrington, Post, and South Streets. My childhood friend Sara from Highland Park recalls the trolley driver stopping on Solvay Street to announce, "Armenian Boulevard, South Solvay." The Armenian Apostolic Church celebrated mass at Zavarian Hall, built in 1929. It was on the corner of Cottrell and Erie Streets, later relocating to the Findlater on West Lafayette and Beard Streets, renamed the Armenian Center (Hye Getron). Across from the Zavarian Hall on Cottrell was the revered Delray Community Center. This multipurpose Tudor Revival edifice was beloved and accommodated the children of immigrants as well as the adult Delray community, with Sunday school, Girl Scouts, piano lessons, cooking lessons, sewing classes, library, and recreational activities. It was built and maintained by the largesse of the Presbyterian Church in the late 1920s and early 1930s.

Delray Italian immigrants had a smaller population and lived interspersed among Armenians and Hungarians on all the streets—Solvay, Cottrell, Green, Harrington, Post, and Schroeder. It is likely that they attended mass at the stately All Saints Catholic Church on Fort Street.

Again moving eastward toward Waterman, Rademacher, Reid, Crawford, and Livernois to Dragoon, the ethnic diversity becomes a very mixed cultural setting, no longer stratified with a predominant group. On South Street, between Rademacher and Crawford, was the very old Cary Elementary School, which we attended and which has since been razed. On the northeast corner of Livernois and South Streets, still recognizable, stands the Slovenian Hall, which served the Slovak people. Judging by many of the street names, it can be assumed that the very early settlers in Delray were of German descent and probably attended the Good Hope Lutheran Church, which still stands on the corner of South and Post Streets.

Farther down the road is Fort Wayne. Technically, Delray can claim Fort Wayne, which was built between 1841 and 1853.[6] This historic fort, off West Jefferson and

---

6 "Historic Fort Wayne," www.michigan.org/property/historic-fort-wayne.

Dragoon Street, was built to protect Detroit from possible British attacks from Windsor's Fort Malden. Currently, it is in great need of repair but still standing.

On the corner of Waterman and Fort Streets is Southwestern High School, dedicated in 1922. This school was honored in 1930 as a fine example of free eclectic Gothic architecture in school design. *The Pageant of America*, a volume on architecture, voiced its opinion on the beauty of this school.[7] This building was planned to be rehabilitated for business use, but currently the plan is in jeopardy because of vandalism. Just down Fort Street, past Waterman, was the James Valentine Campbell Branch Library, built in 1922 and closed in December 1996. It has since been razed. This was my beloved childhood library, where I spent many hours studying and reading, and it was a great resource for multilanguage books.

Many minor ethnic groups and nonimmigrant Americans—Alabama and Kentucky migrants and three or four pockets of black families—were sprinkled in among these Delray streets. This multicultural community was diverse, interesting, colorful, and functioning. This was the Delray I knew and loved.

As recently as 2013, I tried to find some living vestige of the past in the once-buzzing business section of Delray. Lo and behold, on a lonely expanse of West Jefferson looms a red brick building with a large, long hanging sign: "Evinrude Lockeman's Hardware & Boats," with the unexpected "Open Sales and Service." For a nostalgic moment, the sign brought me back to old Delray.

Now a calm has set on the Delray horizon, awaiting a new transition, voiding out the existence of this once historic site. Delray is gone.

---

[7] Talbot Faulkner Hamlin, *The Pageant of America: American Spirit in Architecture* (New Haven: Yale University Press, 1926).

Map of Delray

Delray is located in southwest Detroit, bordering the Detroit River to the south, the Fisher Freeway to the north and west, and Clark Street to the northeast, encompassing approximately 2.9 square miles. In 1930, with the swelling of the immigrant population, Delray grew to roughly 23,000 residents. By 2010, the population had dwindled to fewer than 3,000. In 2018, the future of Delray is uncertain, but the vibrant immigrant community is no more.[1]

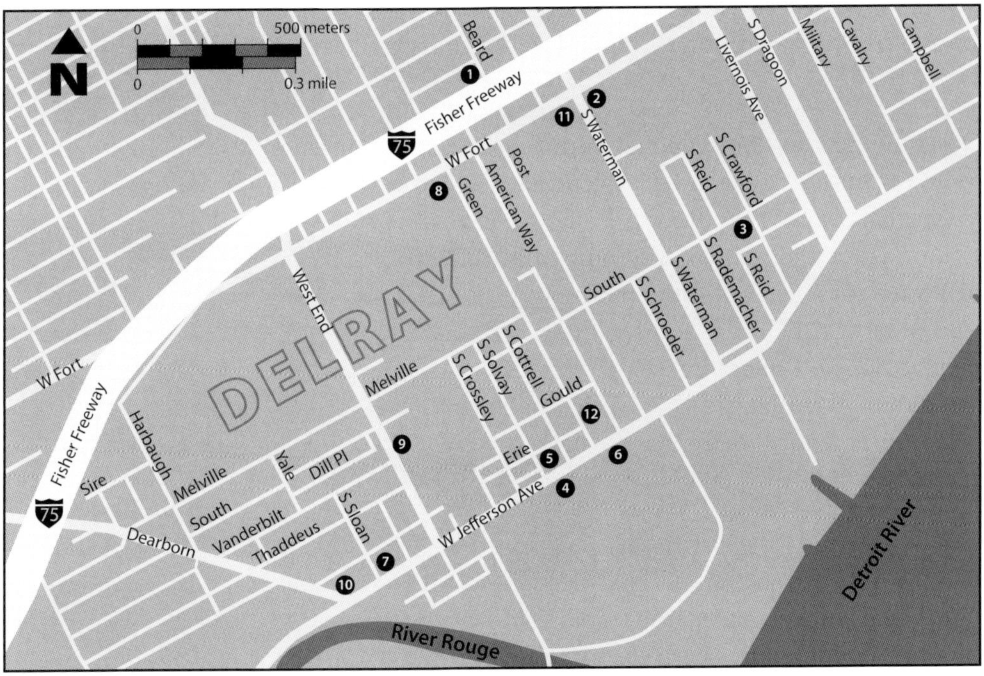

Important Delray Landmarks for the Armenian Immigrant Community

1. Armenian Cultural Center
2. Campbell Branch Library
3. Cary Elementary School
4. Delray Bakery
5. Delray Community Center
6. Delray General Hospital
7. Fancy Pastry Shop
8. Detroit Produce Terminal
9. McMillan Elementary School
10. Neisner Bros., Inc. 5¢ to $1.00
11. Southwestern High School
12. Zavarian Hall

---

1 "Delray, Detroit," https://en.wikipedia.org/wiki/Delray, accessed August 21, 2018.

Prologue 2

MY ARMENIAN DELRAY

"If you don't know where you came from, you won't know where you're going."
– Armenian proverb

In this second prologue, about my Armenian Delray, we catch a glimpse of those early years of the 1930s and 1940s. Growing up in an insular Armenian community was sometimes invasive but always embracing of the American way. These are my own thoughts and memories. Everyone has a story. Every story has a beginning. My story begins in Delray.

We were different. We were Armenian. So what was it like growing up in Delray? My Delray was an Armenian community in southwest Detroit where my immigrant parents had settled, where my father worked at the Union Produce Terminal, and where I was born.

Our Delray colony was not only different, but it was unique. The Armenian immigrants settled and made their homes here, and this was where the first-generation Armenian-Americans were born after the 1915 Genocide. Being of Armenian descent and living in Delray in the early 1930s, after the influx of immigrants from the many regions of Turkish Armenia, meant being different.

My selective child-mind remembers the influence of three realities of being Armenian. First, my parents immigrated to this new country of America and brought with them their "old-country" Armenian culture. So their settlement in Delray became their newly adopted old country. My mother expressed her gratitude with these words in Armenian: "I kiss the soil and drink the water of this great country America for its goodness." During visits to our Armenian neighbors, this same heartfelt gratitude – thanking God for this country – was openly spoken. As a child, I did not comprehend this depth of feeling but interpreted it as an expression of faith, since knowledge of the Genocide was not shared with children.

After the Genocide, Armenians came to America heavily burdened with unbearable and unbelievable grief. My father's cousin Houmayak remembered an incident when, after drinking a glass of beer, my father's repressed anger during a discussion of massacred relatives caused him to crush the glass in his mouth, spewing out the shards with vengeance. He never got over the tragic loss of roughly forty members of his family. For our protection, my father internalized his pain. As children, we were not aware. Our parents rarely talked about the Genocide. It was a hush-hush topic, at times referred to discreetly to protect the children. Much regarding these memories was kept purposely buried in their subconscious minds. Many of my friends recall that when parents revealed something of their Genocide experience, it became too much to bear, resulting in protective amnesia. The story just stopped.

Consequently, I was exposed to two different cultures: I was neither all Armenian nor all American. We, the first generation born as Americans, became known as the "sandwich generation," or, as sociologists term us, "marginal people," those who bridge the gap between two cultures. We were American by birth and Armenian by heritage. Living in this insular Armenian community enriched my life with exposure to loving Delray friends, the Armenian language, culture, and oral history. This rich Armenian background became a cache for collecting Armenian lore, folktales, and proverbs.

The second reality that my child-mind remembers was the tragic murder of Archbishop Leon Tourian in New York City at the Holy Cross Armenian Church in 1933.[1] It was the talk of the town. Delray was plunged into darkness with this news, which caused much sadness, chatter, debate, and angst. The pain brought by this assassination, by a small Armenian revolutionary group, caused a political fracture in our community. It was major news and an added emotional burden on the already stressed Armenian immigrants. I remember the picture of Archbishop Tourian, with his holy scepter, posted on our kitchen wall. I was five, and I remember. This was also the year my brother Mike was born.

The third big reality impressed on my young mind was the busy buzzing among Armenian teenagers about a book, *The Forty Days of Musa Dagh* by Franz Werfel, published in German in 1933 and in English in 1934. This eerie murmuring was about a horrendous atrocity that happened to the Armenian people. It was beyond the ability of my seven-year-old mind to comprehend; I was perplexed and felt detached. I could not grasp it, and it made no sense; this was an abstract, faraway story, unrelated to my life. I can't explain why it affected me to the point where it has remained with me. I vowed to blank out this sad book and never read it. Yet twenty-four years later, with more awareness of the 1915 Armenian Genocide, I had the courage to read this beautifully narrated book about the tragedy. I was

[1] "Archbishop Assassinated in Procession to Altar; Laid to Old-World Feud," *New York Times*, December 25, 1933, p. 1.

awed. How had Franz Werfel grasped the pain and pulse of the Armenian people? He wasn't Armenian!

Among the three memorable events in my life during the 1930s, growing up in Delray stamped the template of my life through heritage, friendship, and exposure to the many Armenian émigrés and their culture. Yes, growing up in Delray was different. I often tell my children how much they have missed. They will never experience the smell of Hungarian doughnuts frying, hear the mellifluous cadence of the Italian language, see the colorful beribboned Polish costumes, hear Gypsy music on the street. They won't smell the aroma of fresh Armenian *gatah* (sweet bread) or the strong *basterma* (spicy meat) spices wafting in the air or hear the old-time storytellers weave their magical tales of the old country—all in one special corner of Detroit called Delray. This added to my interest in and love for Armenian lore, culminating in this collection of Armenian proverbs, sayings, and expressions.

This is what I remember of "old Armenian Delray" from my childhood. Everything that made Delray a functioning community started in the home. It embraced respect for parents and extended to friends and neighbors, always with the supportive tripod of gratefulness, hope, and security of family life. All our friends' mothers were *morqours* (aunts), and the fathers were *barons* (sirs). This emotional bonding with names extended to schoolmates and esoteric nicknames relating to physical or habitual traits: "Chew Fingers," "Banana Nose," "Black Jack," "Harpoon," "Chicken Legs," "Skinny Goon," "Fat Goon," "Goo-Goo Eyes," "Moush," "Stitch," "Mousy," "Doc," "Cheeshod," "Chevy," and others. Our Armenian community was bound together and served as an extended family. Woe to any child apprehended for a misdeed, a school failure, or an altercation with police, and, of course, kudos to any child winning the spelling bee or any academic achievement. Through word of mouth, everyone knew what was going on in our Armenian Delray, which served as a safety valve for behavior, further binding our Armenian community.

Growing up with immigrant parents, whose culture and customs conflicted with the new world, presented challenges to my generation. Dating, for example, was an absolute taboo for daughters of protective fathers. Makeup was an unacceptable display of color distortion. Sleepovers were not part of the traditional family culture. Daughters stayed in their own homes and shared friendships at school and by visiting. Education for daughters was mostly restricted to business classes so they could do office work upon high school graduation. University attendance was not an option. As one father quipped, "College for girls is monkey business." Marriage was the tradition after high school, ideally marriage within the village of the parents. If a man was not from the same village, marrying an Armenian was acceptable. The daughters were more obedient to their parents' rules. The sons were intrigued by blond *odars* (non-Armenians) and had more freedom in their marriage choices. Consequently, becoming Americanized was difficult. At times, the two cultures clashed. And so, as members of the first generation of American Armenians were assimilating, we were losing our Armenian persona. Many tried hard to become Americanized, some changing their names, some denying their ethnicity, yet were never quite in the mainstream. In this process, we never realized the uniqueness of who we were.

Since many parents had limited schooling, their major expectation for their children was a high school diploma. In the immigrants' eyes, this was a monumental accomplishment worthy of much pride. The Armenian children exceeded their parents' aspirations, not only by graduating from high school but also with many continuing on to higher education.

All, or mostly all, of the first generation had Armenian names. We even started kindergarten with these unusual, foreign-sounding names. Mine was Shoushanig. Although it was difficult to pronounce for the non-Armenians, it became a play on words for them: "Shoe shine, shine my shoes." It wasn't hurtful, just funny. Not only did the Armenian kids have ethnic names, but so did the Hungarians and Italians, with Marishka, Erane, Shandon, Angelo, Bruno, and Aldo. Some carried their ethnic names throughout high school. Gradually, our given names were exchanged for their English versions. Mine became Susan. Browsing through my Southwestern High School yearbook, though, I found some who had retained their ethnic names: Haig, Aram, Zaven, Popkin, Sarkis, Nevart, Masis, Dirouhi, and Haygas. Gradually, though, we became Americanized and assimilated into our American culture.

Since our Armenian community was close-knit, we pretty much knew everyone living on the many blocks. What is memorable was the warmth of family and friends when visiting their homes. The Delray Armenian home, rich or poor, had an ingratiating hospitality. The door was always open. Visiting without notice was not frowned upon but acceptable, since phones were not a common utility. In fact, most mothers were prepared for unexpected visitors and maybe somewhat competitive when putting out the best treats at a moment's notice, hoarded for such an occasion. When visiting along with my mother, there was the arched-eyebrow signal telling us whether to partake of candy or goodies. When we were tempted by the candy, our eyes stayed on our mother. An arched eyebrow meant no, because the family may have been poor. Many a sticky Christmas candy was enjoyed in summer. During one visit to my mother's friend, I was introduced to a pink-colored drink. This supposed Armenian treat, called *shooroup*, was whipped up in a jiffy for refreshment on a hot summer day. Even now, I can't stand this sweet rose syrup drink. Memory brings tears to my eyes when I remember an invitation to a friend's house for supper. With this large family, I shared a bowl of beans. I've never forgotten this humble meal; it filled me with love. Looking back, it was obvious that hospitality was an indigenous trait of the Armenian home and a reflection of the humble generosity of the Armenian mother during those bleak, difficult years.

Armenian home life traditionally seemed patriarchal, but that was in name only. Behind the scenes, the matriarch was the gear that put the family in motion. Quietly, the mother was in control. Since fathers were gone for the day, mothers had the responsibility of running the home on a tight budget, food shopping and preparation, guiding and disciplining the children, and maybe caring for elderly parents. To make ends meet, some took in boarders, as there were many bachelors in Delray during the Depression years. When I look back, the realization hits me that our mothers were so young, in their twenties, thirties, and forties, yet they looked so old. They acted old and dressed old. Their floral-patterned house dresses were the attire of the day, and they wore oxford tied shoes, with lisle hose twisted into a magical knot at the knee to hold up the stocking. Aprons were an added cover for much work to be done. Since carrying a purse was not always convenient, money was hidden in the bosom for quick transactions. Both of my best friends' mothers were in their forties, and my impression was that they were ancient. But one has to remember that they came to America with heavy hearts, and dressing fashionably was not a top priority, but rather clothing was a matter of comfort; being stylish was not a consideration. I do remember one occasion when an Armenian woman came to visit with her five-year-old daughter. She had on a pale blue suit, rather rare for those times. Her visit was prompted by need—to borrow money for her daughter's medical procedure. My mother looked at her and asked, "Is that a new suit?" "Yes," she answered. My mother then responded, "If you have money for a new suit, you have money for the doctor." I was surprised. My mother usually saved for such circumstances and was generous, but she was also judicious. She balanced the scales and didn't help.

In Delray, the family was the bedrock of security, and Armenian food was the magnet for gatherings at family tables, friends' homes, picnics, and wherever one could sit and enjoy a social meeting. Since these foods required special ingredients for dolma, *boreg* (baked filled pastries), pilaf, baklava, and other dishes, Armenian grocery stores sprang up on many corners—some across from each other, some around the corner, all in close proximity and within short walking distance. This was a great advantage for Armenian mothers and cooks. While the fathers were working, the mothers had time to chitchat with friends and neighbors while completing errands for staples such as *gorgot* (skinless whole-wheat grain), bulgur, lentils, tahine, parsley, rice, and *pedeh* (oval bread) for supper. I remember waiting patiently while my mother and her friends would jokingly relate inside family stories (in Armenian, of course). One such tale was that my immigrant uncle went to the store for sugar and remembered the logo had Xs on the box. Not knowing the English word for sugar, he knew that Xs meant kisses. So he blew kisses to the horrified salesgirl, hoping she'd understand. Fortunately, another shopper explained his need for sugar to the confused employee.

These stores were small and family-operated. One staple that was never purchased was yogurt (*madzoon*). In those days, yogurt was not a commercial product, and our mothers often boiled milk to make the next batch. Yogurt needs a starter (*magart*). So it was common to go to the neighbors', cup in hand, for the starter. You couldn't make yogurt without it. If the *magart* was sour, direction was given to go to another neighbor with the emblematic "beggar's cup" to be filled with the yogurt starter.

On West Jefferson were Kumjian's Independent Grocers and Laktzian's Grocery Store; on Solvay were Mashco's Meat Market and George's Roosevelt Grocery; on Cottrell was Maneal's (Tarpinian), across the street was a Keghi-villager-owned grocery store, and down the street, on the corner of Erie, was Topalian's Grocery Store. North on Green Street was Takvor's General Store across from the Produce Terminal. On Fort Street was Karnig Charchian's Grocery Store, across from Southwestern High School. Besides these Armenian supply stores, George Simon's (non-Armenian/Bulgarian) Delray Bakery fulfilled customers' needs with the best *pedeh* in the world at the corner of Cottrell and West Jefferson. Although Delray Bakery was not Armenian-owned, it was an important part of the Delray Armenian food tradition. During World War II, Delray lost its share of young Armenian sons. The returning veterans were celebrated by some families with a *madagh* (offering/ sacrifice) feast and a thanksgiving sacrifice of a lamb for their safe return. The whole lamb was baked in the huge bakery's oven and was shared with neighbors.

Being in the produce business, my father supplied potatoes to grocery stores, an important product for his livelihood. We were very familiar with the sight of my dad lugging a hundred-pound bag of potatoes to the stores. One day he brought home a burlap sack and lightly and gently placed it on the floor. My mother exclaimed, in Armenian, "What are we going to do with all these potatoes?" In the 1930s, a few small businesses were experimenting with snack uses for potatoes. One such entrepreneur was an east-side Detroit Italian immigrant who was testing my father's product in his basement. The tasty result of this was delivered in a huge burlap sack filled with delicious homemade potato chips. Needless to say, my brothers and I savored this addictive treat in a marathon eating binge and forever became potato chip devotees. My immigrant father was becoming an American businessman without losing his Armenian identity.

My father also made available an abundance of other produce, such as watermelon. In our home, watermelon was much enjoyed, especially by my brother George. He was five years old and in kindergarten. In the 1930s, everyone came home from school for lunch. One afternoon, the safety patrol came to the door and announced to my mother, "Lady, your son had a b-i-i-i-g accident!" For a young Armenian immigrant mother, the word *accident* set off a flurry of fear and anxiety. With her limited English comprehension and her bewilderment, my mother expressed in her trembling voice, "What you say, ax-ee-dent?" The word aroused terrifying thoughts, and she reacted accordingly. "Lady, look in his pants!" the safety patrol boy answered with half a smile. Sure enough, eating too much watermelon had consequences. With grateful relief, she remedied it with a quick cleanup and a bath. Family life proceeded in the new world of America with unexpected happenings.

With hindsight, it is obvious that the Armenians of Delray were well supplied for their food needs and functioned as an independent community. Judging from the number of Armenian grocery stores on Solvay and Cottrell Streets, one can conclude that food was a priority in the Armenian home.

In addition to the cluster of grocery stores were the Zavarian Hall and the Delray Community Center on Cottrell. The Zavarian Hall was a multipurpose structure that also served as an Armenian church, school, library, coffee house, and venue for cultural events, weddings, and funerals. This was a haven for the Armenian community. As children, we would attend the Armenian church, where my two brothers served as candle holders and were often reprimanded by the priest for inattention—playfully swaying the candle holders from side to side, interrupting the priest's vision for scripture reading. I could hear his scolding voice reminding them of their churchless behavior. After church, we would run across the street to the Delray Community Center for Sunday school.

Delray's "Little Armenia" was very fortunate to have this beautiful red brick Tudor Revival edifice to serve the many needs of the neighborhood, built by the Presbyterian Church around 1930. It was a multifunctional facility and extended self-help resources to the Delray community. Miss Ethel McKinsey, headmistress, took charge with noble reins and harnessed goals, by setting up programs for all nationalities in the Delray community to aid and acquaint the émigré families in the American way of life. Miss McKinsey poured her heart and soul into this project; it was a challenge and a full-time job. Fortunately, she had living quarters on the premises. With her competent skills in organization and implementation, she succeeded in setting up sewing groups with donated yarn, thread, and needles, as well as cooking classes to familiarize the women with utensils and American cooking. We could smell unfamiliar foods with pungent odors, like pork and beans. For us, it was *odar* (foreign) food. I remember the women seated in the main hall discussing current social concerns. My mother wanted to voice her thoughts but couldn't. Her English was not comprehensible, and I was anxious for her.

Then there was Sunday school. Trained teachers were brought in from the Presbyterian Church, under the supervision of Mr. Millar, a beloved Christian leader. This was not an easy task, setting up specific programs for the different age groups to make it workable and enjoyable. I loved my Sunday school classes held in this beautiful setting with the multipaned front window. I couldn't wait for the next weekly lesson pamphlet with its Bible story. In the center hall were many pictures depicting biblical stories. As a child, I related to them and, in my naive and finite mind and heart, believed they were all Armenians, even Jesus. One wintry Sunday, which was bitterly cold and blustery, my father's car wouldn't start. Against my mother's advice, I walked five blocks to Sunday school, my face numb from the extreme weather. I wanted to know more about the "prodigal son," a parable I didn't understand. To my disappointment, there was one teacher at the door—no classes. Certainly, this Presbyterian Sunday school impacted my life with Bible teachings. Later, the high schoolers were trained to teach, and Susie Hoogasian Villa was my teacher.

It would be kind to say the Armenian boys needed discipline, always jumpy and boisterous. Miss McKinsey was familiar with the rambunctious and vigorous boys in our community. It was a great idea to channel this energy constructively. The second floor was the ideal venue for athletic expression, so the huge gymnasium became the playing field for the great sport of basketball. We could hear the thumping and dribbling of the ball and cries of triumph when someone made a basket. In March 1946, Southwestern High School won the championship basketball game at Olympia Stadium.

In addition to the services already mentioned, we had Girl Scout classes, piano lessons, hobby classes, recreational programs, adult language classes, public health services, and a small library—all without fees. This was where Miss McKinsey forced me to dial a telephone for the first time—quite a frightening experience for one who had never handled a telephone. Adding to the new experiences at the Community Center were piano lessons, taught by Mrs. Jones, our black teacher from the Delray neighborhood. My friend Irene and I looked forward to practicing on cardboard folding keyboards without ever hearing the notes. Summertime brought the pleasure of reading the Honey Bunch series and Nancy Drew mysteries from the small library. An even greater adventure was Kiwanis Camp at Lake Orion, Michigan. This was where we learned to swim, hike, shoot with bow and arrow, make handicrafts, and do group singing in fireside programs. At camp, the only downside for me was the strange food, especially creamed corn, which never remained in my stomach. How very privileged we were, with all that was provided by the largesse of the Presbyterian Church. Recently, my friend Marian said, "At Kiwanis camp was the best food and the best time of those Depression years." Looking back, I see that we were not cognizant of all the goodness and useful services heaped on us by the Delray Community Center. It was a center for everyone and for all seasons. We were very fortunate.

While we had many activities at the Community Center, we also had fun times at home and in the neighborhood. Of course, we walked everywhere—to our neighbors, school, Sunday school, theater, and stores. Everything was accessible. This made our neighborhood ripe for human bonding, a lost lifestyle today.

At home, our activities and entertainment were simple. After school and on Saturdays and Sundays, we participated in homey activities such as hopscotch, pick-up sticks, jacks, marbles, yo-yos, or cutting out pictures of popular movie stars like Shirley Temple, Jane Withers, and Sonja Henie. Without the convenience of telephones, we would go to our friends' houses to call on them. I smile when I remember calling my friend and sing-songing, "Roo-zie, come on out and play." If it was rainy or cold, we played dominoes indoors. Outside, we also played "tin can alley." We crushed tin cans to fit our shoes and would clang loudly down the alley to play tag or races. The larger the can, the louder the noise as we stomped in the alley.

Prologue 2

Besides the activities at home, on the street, and at the Community Center, another source of entertainment was the popular Grande Theater. It had two sections. The first, facing West Jefferson, was the entrance, with an impressive, long polished-brass rail separating the entering patrons from the popcorn and treat aisle. Then one would proceed across the alley to the projection area. Weekends brought flocks of excited children, especially on Saturdays, to view the Clutching Hand, Buck Rogers, and Dick Tracey serials. Admission sometimes was a canned-food donation. Sundays, after church and Sunday school, we spent the whole afternoon viewing the same movies two or three times. My brother George often stayed and returned home alone. We were consumed with the fantasy world of cowboys—Gene Autry, Tom Mix, and Roy Rogers with his horse, Trigger. My only anxiety at the movies was seeing the MGM roaring lion, which growled at the audience before the start of the movie. For me, the shining star of the 1930s silver screen was the endearing Shirley Temple. It is said that this mite of a child raised the morale of the Depression years with her flawless tap-dancing, singing, and audacious performances in many movies. She mesmerized us into the world of innocent make-believe. We, her contemporaries, wanted to look like her, to dress like her with a flouncing polka-dot dress, and to have layers of bouncing banana curls. My mother tried twirling my hair, then wrapping each curl with strips of cotton. Mine never looked like Shirley's mop of layered curls. While we young ones loved the floppy banana curls, adults wanted the glamour of dual pompadour hairstyles mimicking stars like Joan Crawford.

In the 1930s and '40s, the silver screen engrossed not only the young but also the immigrant adults. One cannot forget the glitzy Hollywood panoramic productions, dazzling with white furs, sparkling sequins, jewelry, and glamorous satin evening gowns. Though language may have been a barrier, the amazing visual effects didn't need words, a far cry from the actual situation of those years. The Grande Theater was a welcome escape into the world of fantasy, with the musicals of Nelson Eddy and Jeanette MacDonald, Fred Astaire and Ginger Rogers, and the Ziegfeld Follies; tear-jerking love stories with Joan Crawford, Bette Davis, and Jean Harlow; and all-day Saturday serials. Movies were a soothing balm and an illusionary diversion from reality which transformed the weary Depression years into an uplifting experience. To this day, I enjoy the reruns of the black-and-white movies of that era which somehow tugged at the heartstrings with their simple emotional messages that the immigrants understood. Those movies worked for those times.

Prologue 2

Today television is our home entertainment; in the '30s and '40s, it was the radio. We would be glued to our precious Philco radio, listening to *The Hermit's Cave*, a spooky mystery program, on Sunday night. My younger brother would hide under the bed, he was so frightened. After school on Monday, we looked forward to another episode of *Jack Armstrong, The All American Boy*, sponsored by Wheaties. Then, on Friday, was the ever-enthralling *The Green Hornet*. And there was *The Shadow*, introduced with the pithy words "Who knows what evil lurks in the hearts of men? Only the Shadow knows!" On Saturday evening was *Your Hit Parade*. We knew all the songs and usually sang along, with song sheets purchased at Neisner Bros. We were consumed with these radio serials, our mothers loved the soap operas, and our fathers always followed the evening newscasts. When the news came on, my father demanded absolute silence, and my brothers and I respected him by playing quietly.

We had activities in the home, in the Community Center, and outside, but there was a different beat and sound on the Delray streets. There was a rhythm of voices and sounds of movement of carts and horses and occasionally cars. There were the horse-drawn food peddlers, melodically singing "Bee-na-no, bee-na-no . . . yel-loow pea-cheess," attracting the housewives to the produce carts for supplies. The alley peddler, trotting slowly with his overaged horse, called people to buy their scrap-metal housewares, and the Wayne Creamery milkman's wagon, whose horse clip-clopped along, deposited fertilizer cakes to be picked up by the many gardeners. The milkman would deliver the glass-bottled milk on the porches. In the winter, the cream would raise the circular seal above the opening, and it became an "iced cream" treat for us.

The summers always seemed hot and dusty in Delray. Refrigerators were not common, so iceboxes served to keep food cold. The icebox usually had three openings, one for the ice and two for storage. So the ice truck chug-chugging along, delivering ice blocks, was followed by a parade of thirsty children, begging for ice shards to quench their thirst. Also enticing these kids on the sidewalks was the ice cream cart. It was a white rectangular box, hand-pushed and rolled along on two large spindled wheels, filled with popsicles and cold treats wrapped in silver foil. Always a bunch of kids would trail behind the strolling cart to get a three-cent treat. Now the sounds of horses, wagons, and cart wheels are gone. That was then . . . the Delray I knew as a child.

Another usual Delray street activity was pursued around the corner from Cottrell, on the southern end of Solvay, in the well-known strip of Armenian coffee houses known as *sourjarans*. The many single and widowed men residing in Delray found food, lodging, and friendship in these havens. Many married men also found these coffee houses, or what we would now call man caves, to be a respite from work and a place for fellowship with friends; a place to share memories, to play cards, and to enjoy Armenian *sourj* (thick, black coffee), while playing *tavloo* (backgammon). Many a child went looking for his or her father, uncle, or brother when he didn't show up at home after work. The likely place of discovery was the Armenian coffee house. These places survived into the 1960s.

While the Delray street scenes were noisy with horses, carts, ice trucks, and cars, there was a quieter activity taking place on the many porches. Almost every house had a porch along the street, a natural architectural appendage of these early-1900s homes. The porches differed in appearance: some were elongated across the house front, some were extended on the side, a few had a gazebo-like extension with stairs leading to the sidewalk, and some just had a cozy sitting area. The houses were built close together, sometimes separated by a cement walk, so window shades would be drawn for privacy. These porches were like a linked fence, meshing the families together and serving as an open communication center for talking, hearing neighborhood gossip, exchanging recipes, sharing old-country stories and sometimes a Genocide remembrance. One summer afternoon, while gently catnapping on my mother's lap, unbeknownst to my mother's friend, I heard my first Genocide story. I was seven, and it still prods my memory never to forget. Certainly, porches were a factor in binding the neighborhood, served a vital social need, and at times provided a cathartic relief for the immigrants' past pain. It was here, in such a place as Delray, that oral tradition flourished. While movies served as a distraction from reality, the porches served as a venue for sharing human experiences in reality. This was an "exchange platform" for rich interpersonal relationships.

Why am I writing about porches? Even the word *porch* sounds old-fashioned today. The simple answer is that this house appendage was an important gathering place in the Delray community and served as a catalyst to bind the immigrant peoples within the neighborhood. It was the center for socializing and uniting a fractured people in a new world. Now the value of porches for cohesive neighborhoods has brought new attention and interest from community developers. With this hindsight—"Neo-traditionalists [remember] towns when houses were so close you could pop over to borrow butter, when owners mingled naturally on the street, when kids could run up and down the sidewalks, where every home has a big front porch so residents can chat with neighbors"[2]—adding porches has been a compelling idea. This is the Delray I knew. What's old is now becoming a new concept for an old-fashioned neighborhood lifestyle. It is happening here in Michigan in some suburban Detroit communities. Today there is a recognized need for such communities, with porches, to make neighborhoods more congenial. Porches in Delray served a meaningful purpose when life was simple, personal, and accessible, and they were instrumental in giving voice and identity to the Armenian immigrant.

Delray was a special place to live and grow up, rooted in rich ethnic culture and nurturing lasting childhood friendships. Exposure to other cultures was another enriching experience in this neighborhood. Humility abounded in our outlook, which was a reflection of our parents' values. As children, we felt a leap of joy from the simplest events of our lives. Despite those trying years, our cup was half full, and the memories of Delray are good ones.

Life was getting more palatable; America was becoming home. During the 1940s, Delray families started to migrate to the outlying neighborhoods—north of Fort Street, to northwest Detroit, and south to Allen Park, and Lincoln Park. By the 1970s, Armenian Delray had become a blur of the past. New Apostolic churches were built, St. John's Apostolic Church in Southfield and St. Sarkis and the Armenian Catholic Church in Dearborn. The Armenian Congregational Church relocated to Southfield from Detroit. Armenian families by this time had successfully assimilated into the American culture.

I hope these scenes of old Delray give a picture of an old-world experience, gradually assimilating into the new world of America. This picture of old-world Delray comes from my childhood memories and is true to my experiences. Life in this Delray enclave inspired my passion for collecting Armenian proverbs and lore. The home was the beginning, where proverbs were used to teach and advise, extending to hearing tales from family, friends, and neighbors, and culminating in this collection of oral history as heard until the present time.

These prologues about Delray have been purposely staged to set up the background for my collection of Armenian proverbs, sayings, and expressions. Delray was the stage, the Armenian immigrant was the star, and I was the audience—listening, recording, and collecting Armenian oral history.

---

2 Judy Rose, "Welcome to the Neighborhood," *Detroit Free Press*, December 22, 2013, p. F1.

Introduction

DEFINITIONS AND ORIGINS OF PROVERBS

"Proverbs are part of the country's social glue."
– Wolfgang Mieder
Professor of German and folklore
University of Vermont

Welcome to the world of Armenian proverbs. Armenian proverbs are important—they have historical relevance, human interest, wisdom of word, and strength of endurance. They reveal much about the spirit of a people and their culture. My observation of this collection is that Armenian proverbs are a mirror of village life and reflect the people's faith, struggles, and priorities. This customary "word-of-mouth" tradition was an effective, homey, understandably familiar method: to teach, advise, admonish, inspire, and, at times, entertain. It was the glue that bonded the family together with a like-minded lifestyle and similar expectations.

First, we need a definition. What is a proverb? For the purposes of this book, I give a spiritual, academic, folkloric, and folksy definition.

The Bible says that the purpose of the proverbs of Solomon is "for gaining wisdom and instruction; for understanding words of insight; for receiving instruction in prudent behavior, doing what is right and just and fair; for giving prudence to those who are simple, knowledge and discretion to the young."[1] Dictionary.com defines a proverb as "a short popular saying, usually of unknown and ancient origin, that expresses effectively some commonplace truth or useful thought; adage; saw."

According to folklorist Jan Harold Brunvand, "The true proverb is always a complete sentence, varies slightly in form, and usually expresses some general truth or wisdom."[2] Another folklorist, Archer Taylor, wrote, "A proverb is a saying current among the folk."[3] And the medieval writer Moses ibn Ezra said, "A proverb has three characteristics: few words, good sense, and a fine image."[4]

1 Proverbs 1: 1–4 (New International Version).
2 Jan Harold Brunvand, *The Study of American Folklore*, 4th ed. (New York: W. W. Norton, 1998), p. 75.
3 Archer Taylor, *The Proverb* (Copenhagen: Rosenkilde and Bagger, 1962), p. 3.
4 Quoted in Shirley Kumove, *More Words, More Arrows* (Detroit: Wayne State University Press, 1999), p. 21.

In reviewing these definitions, key words pop up that adequately validate the many collected Armenian proverbs by using wisdom and instruction in prudence, right, and justice; commonplace, general truth, useful thought; few words, good sense, and fine image; and currency of relatedness to the common folk. Finally, Shirley Kumove states: "At this point, it is worth reminding ourselves that a folk saying is an expression transmitted orally from one person to another, containing a summation of spiritual, cultural and ethical values."[5] The Armenian proverbs validate all of these definitions and prove that they work even today.

What is revealed in this Armenian proverb collection? From the beginning, it becomes obvious that there is a familiarity, an understandable common language, which was a vital and direct means of connecting with all household members. This implies that life was simple and supports the value of the spoken word, whether in imparting advice, teaching, or entertaining with folktales or narratives about village happenings. Accordingly, Taylor claimed that proverbs fall into two categories: "learned" or "popular."[6] The learned proverbs have a literary tradition, from the classics or the Bible, and the popular proverbs stem from everyday language. This is true of almost all the proverbs in this collection, where the usual common language was layman *(ashkharapar)* as opposed to academic, ancient, classical Armenian *(krapar)*. Through this everyday language, proverbs thrived in the villages and could be known as conversational folklore.

What is striking and evident in these Armenian proverbs is that day-to-day issues come to the forefront and tell us about the villagers' faith, struggles, and priorities. Education was minimal, so the most powerful communicating tool was the spoken word, and the most effective message was the proverb with a few pithy words. Hence the prevalence of much Armenian conversational lore was understandable, directed, applicable, idealistic, related, and often moralistic in the situation.

FAITH OF THE VILLAGER

Teaching members of a large household depended solely on word-of-mouth information. Mindful that the church was the hub of the village and Christianity was the spiritual heart of the Armenian people, the Bible was the influential teaching resource. What was learned came from church attendance: hearing scripture verses, Bible parables, and homilies which were repeated at home and used situationally

5 Kumove, *More Words, More Arrows*, p. 21.
6 Taylor, *The Proverb*, p. 44.

for teaching, advising, and directing children and the household. Faith was the instrumental creed for living, and the Bible was the text. This worked, and there are many Armenian proverbs that evolved from the biblical printed word, such as:

- *Biblical proverb:* "But a rod is for the back of one who has no sense." (Proverbs 10: 13)

  Armenian proverb: "He who does not hear with his ears will hear with his back."

- *Biblical proverb:* "Those who humble themselves will be exalted." (Matthew 23: 12)

  Armenian proverb: "He who humbles himself shall be exalted."

- *Biblical proverb:* "And be content with what you have." (Hebrews 13: 5)

  Armenian proverb: "He who is content with his lot is the world's happiest man."

- *Biblical proverb:* "Make up your mind not to put any stumbling block or obstacle in the way of a brother or sister." (Romans 14: 13)

  Armenian proverb: "A rock is placed in front of your knee."

- *Biblical proverb:* "A prophet has no honor in his own country." (John 4: 44)

  Armenian proverb: "An honest man is thrown out of forty villages."

- *Biblical proverb:* "Can a man scoop fire into his lap without his clothes being burned?" (Proverbs 6: 27)

  Armenian proverb: "Where the fire falls, there it burns."

- *Biblical proverb:* "It is better to heed the rebuke of a wise person than to listen to the song of fools." (Ecclesiastes 7: 5)

  Armenian proverb: "It's better to have intelligent enemies than foolish friends."

And the biblical references can go on and on, as there are many more parallels between the Bible and Armenian sayings.

Fortunately, I received this knowledge through my unlettered mother-in-law, who was born in the nineteenth century. She was one of my invaluable sources, with a mind that had fragmented channels to the present but remembered details of her early years quite lucidly. Her mind compensated for her lack of reading and writing skills by becoming a repository and keeper of memories. She drew on this information as a communication tool. The authenticity of her sayings and stories is reliable because the repetitions seldom varied; her words and descriptions were always the same. Actually, her mind became a conduit for the spoken word through proverbs, folk stories, and folk medicine. She passed down many biblical words of wisdom, and this oral information has been a lifeline to the preservation of Armenian proverbs and lore. The honed skill of rote memory in this uneducated woman, and most likely all villagers, is an amazing phenomenon. One can conclude that the Armenian villager has been instrumental in perpetuating the continuance of oral tradition. There is a Polish proverb that applies well to the wisdom of these villagers: "The peasant is a born philosopher; the aristocrat must learn to be one." Susie Hoogasian Villa echoed this in her observation that "villagers retain the oldest pattern of Armenian oral history."

STRUGGLES OF THE VILLAGER

We know that the Bible was effective and influential in the lives of the Armenian villager. We also know through many proverbs about the villagers' economic and social struggles, as indicated by their stringent existence under dominant Turkish rule. Armenian peasants needed to live frugally and wisely and always to plan ahead. Consequently, they were not wasteful people; everything had a useful purpose. Substantiating this hardship, Villa notes, "Life was difficult for the Armenian, for not only was the heavy Turkish taxation a great problem to the villager, he was in constant terror of raids and pillage."[7] Their existence was inundated with events. The following proverbs reflect some of the struggles of the Armenian people under Turkish rule:

- "Walk narrowly during wide (ample) days, so you can walk widely during your narrow (lean) days."
- "Roll your quilt according to the length of your feet."
- "Where bread, there tread."

[7] Susie Hoogasian Villa, *100 Armenian Tales* (Detroit: Wayne State University Press, 1966), p. 37.

- "Don't drop your sugar in the water."
- "Keep your door closed, so you won't catch your neighbor at thievery."
- "When the peasant is poor, the country is poor."
- "The Armenian can draw water from a stone."
- "Don't step into the water unless you can see the bottom."
- "The snake, which is a snake, measures the soil he eats."
- "Hope is the bread of the unfortunate."

PRIORITIES OF THE VILLAGER

The Armenian villagers' lives were hard, but their priorities were simple. Despite their daily struggles in a hostile environment, their survival skills of resourcefulness, resilience, and prudence placed them in a position to succeed. With their bedrock faith and church, they were able to sustain the welfare of the extended family and to continue their ancestral culture, the pivotal center always being the family and its priorities. Scanning through the many proverbs, it becomes obvious that this daunting journey through life was all about coping with everyday concerns. The proverbs expose the exigencies of their lives from cradle to grave and their priorities to nurture the extended family.

Through word-of-mouth and face-to-face instruction, the proverb was an effective means of communicating. It was the messenger that worked to reveal the important matters of life. My personal observation finds these family priorities to be as follows:

- Advising and teaching: "Let what I say be an earring on your ear; don't forget it."
- Awareness: "All who laugh in your face are not your friends."
- Faith: "When God gives, He gives with two hands."
- Family: "If the child is not spanked, the knee will be slapped."
- Gratefulness: "The hen, which is a hen, when drinking water looks up (to heaven)."

- Inspiration: "In every person's heart lies hidden a hero."
- Learning: "Even if you know a thousand things, ask the person who knows only one."
- Marriage: "When buying cloth, look at the selvage; when marrying a girl, look at the mother."
- Morality: "One shame for the beggar, a double shame for the nongiver."
- Respect: "The donkey, which is a donkey, will bow its head when the church bell chimes."

When reviewing this proverb collection, I recall that using a proverb served a meaningful purpose in exposing the human condition and enlightening the situation with simplicity and awareness. Occasionally, when a friend or I would use a proverb in a social setting, for example, it was not unusual for a third party to chime in, "That's not the way I remember it." According to R. G. Bayan, "It might appear that the proverb has been distorted, but on closer examination—gentle reader—it will be found to possess the charm, to the people, into whose tongue it has been translated; imparted by, and stamped with the skill, and genius of the translator, hence its newness of form is no deterioration from its original piquancy of style."[8]

It is also important to consider the many variables that contribute to a proverb: Are the people from the same Armenian village or perhaps a small town or large city? Was the proverb stated by someone who spoke a different dialect? Because the exact words are not being used, or the words are in a different order, that does not invalidate the proverb. What is actually being transmitted is the fact that "whenever a proverb is remembered and spoken," the original culture and language are alive and still relevant today.

Just before this book went to press, a proverb fell into my lap that hints at the everyday preoccupations challenging man until his death. It is an appropriate proverb with which to end this introduction, because it inclusively interprets man's travail—life—on earth and why: "God gives man a thousand and one encumbrances so he will not be preoccupied with death." A good proverb gives life to words and gives meaning to life in a few simple words.

---

[8] Special thanks to Hagop D. Mouradian for sharing R. G. Bayan, *Armenian Proverbs and Sayings* (trans.), 4th ed. (Venice: Academy of S. Lazarus, 1932).

Methodology

COLLECTING OF PROVERBS

"The genius, wit, and the spirit of a nation are discovered by their proverbs."
– Francis Bacon

Since this section of the book is about collecting proverbs, it is important to acknowledge when collecting began and who did it.[1]

Paremiography is the Greek word that defines the process as "the study of collecting and writing of proverbs." The earliest recorded collector of proverbs was Desiderius Erasmus Roterodamus, a Dutch humanist, writer, and theologian and a masterful collector of Greek and Latin adages during the Renaissance period.

His most famous and monumental proverb collection is called *Adagiorum chiliades (Thousands of Proverbs)*, with 4,151 entries, published in 1508. This proverb collection has been described as "the oldest book in the world."[2] However, it was an earlier published collection known as the *Adagio* that had a profound influence on readers. These printed proverbs soon permeated Europe's varied languages and were adapted and translated into their particular ethnic usage, which then became part of their cultural lore. It would be fair to say that Erasmus affected the oral tradition of many countries with his seminal source of proverbs. This could be relevant to many Armenian collections and could apply to this one. True enough, I found Armenian proverbs from Erasmus's short list, probably attributed to *Adagio*:

- Crocodile tears: *Gogorteelosee artsoonk guh tapeh.*
- To squeeze water out of a stone: *(Hayeruh) Karen choor guh hanen.*

---

1 Some of this discussion is based on information from Peter Unseth, "How to Collect 1,000 Proverbs Quickly: Field Methods for Eliciting and Collecting Proverbs," Graduate Institute of Applied Linguistics and SIL International, www.gial.edu/documents/gialens/Vol1-1/Unseth-Proverbs-article.pdf, accessed April 13, 2018; and Samantha Berman, "Proverbs with a Bonus," *Folklore* 63: 154–155. The latter is a review of Edward Zelem, *Zarbul Masalha: 151 Afghan Dari Proverbs*, 3rd ed. (Tampa: Cultures Direct Press, 2015).

2 Roumyana Petrova, "Introduction to Paremiology,"in *A Comprehensive Guide to Proverb Studies* (Berlin: De Gruyter, 2014), pp. 243–261.

- He blows his own trumpet: *Eerehn duduguh guh chaleh.*
- Like father, like son: *(Duhghan) Keetehn unger eh.*

In fact, I used the Armenian proverb "He blows his own horn" upon hearing a speaker boasting at a funeral. In this instance, you could also apply the apt proverb "Go die, come (back), then I will love you." (*Kuhnah mereer, yegoor seerem.*).

History confirms Erasmus as the father of collecting and printing proverbs. Now, fast-forward to the twenty-first century, hundreds of years since Erasmus's publications. There is evidence that proverbs are alive and well and effectively used in homes, lectures, classrooms, church podiums, and elsewhere to enlighten the listener. Certainly, this was true of my exposure to Armenian conversational lore in these venues, and this was the source of my word-of-mouth sayings in this collection. Erasmus's seminal concept of collecting and printing may largely be responsible for the survival of proverbs. Credit goes to him for the fact that proverbs are still spoken, collected, and printed. Armenians benefited, and their proverbs have survived and served the people well.

Where did this Armenian collection take root, and how did it start? It all began in the home. Since entertainment was limited in the 1930s, sharing stories at home and during visits to friends became an enjoyable pastime, easing the mood of this difficult period. Conversational sharing of lore seemed to be an inherent talent of the old-timers. Delray had some wondrous narrators who kept us spellbound with tales that could begin with "There was and there wasn't…" (*Gar oo cheegar…*) or "It happened and it didn't happen…" (*Eghav oo cheghav…*). Each of these stories often ended with a pithy proverb to validate the tale. Also memorable is the use of proverbs related to everyday happenings—in short, teaching with a few words to make a point, seemingly a throwback to an old-world generational teaching method, and the spoken word was effective.

Sharing stories in our home, my mother also used situational proverbs to admonish and teach, folk stories to retain the past, humorous anecdotes to entertain, stories of acts of heroism and triumph to inspire, and descriptions of folk medicine for natural healing—all attributed to her grandmother Mayrakhan, who raised her. I could relate to my great-grandmother through these stories. She was my heroine, and I bonded with her through her folktales and her loving care of my mother. Mayrakhan was a wonder woman who was ahead of her time, working with her husband, a doctor, aiding in medical treatment, prescribing herbal medicine, and embalming bodies for burial. After her daughter's (my grandmother's) untimely passing, Mayrakhan assumed responsibility for raising her grandchildren, my mother and her siblings. So we inherited a doubly rich background in Armenian oral tradition from our mother and from Delray. Being born in America, I found this old-world wisdom fascinating and at times mind-boggling and unbelievable, and it opened up an unknown vista into a past culture. This exposure led me to jot down what interested my curious mind, and my Delray exposure was an added bonus as a source of colloquial stories and proverbs. My childhood was alive with folksy lore; those years were raw with emotions—living, caring, and sharing. This process served as a conduit or vehicle that enabled me to collect and preserve a limited part of my heritage. Ever since, I've logged and chronicled proverbs.

One might ask how I collected. My response would be: with opportunity and timely luck. Let me explain. To collect the spoken word, you need an opportune situation that may evoke a timely proverb. I borrowed a bit of relevant wisdom from *100 Armenian Tales* by Susie Hoogasian Villa. She claims that oral tradition lies dormant in the memory of folk, ready for quick recall, and with proper stimulation can evoke a traditional folktale.[3]

Always aware that a proverb might pop up, I would keep a pen handy. Upon hearing an Armenian proverb, my hearing would perk up, my eyes would light up, and joyfully, in my nonacademic, phonetic Armenian, I would scribble the saying on any available scrap of paper—envelope flaps, church bulletins, newspaper corners, napkins, grocery bags, whatever—fearful of missing a single word of what was said. And it worked. The urgency of the situation lent itself to this frantic method of collecting. Proverbs were collected, as spoken, from Armenians in all walks of life: survivors and displaced immigrants of the 1915 Armenian Genocide, family, friends, educated informers, unlettered villagers, casual bystanders, and even TV (specifically, the series *Mannix*, which starred Mike Connors, whose birth name was Krikor Ohanian).

Ideally, Armenian venues are fertile grounds for reaping Armenian lore; many invaluable proverbs were unearthed at bazaars, lectures, church services, and social gatherings (*khunchooks*), all of which can be loaded with chatter and humming with people. So it happened at one of these social events that I was asked, "Sue, give me a proverb!" For a dazed moment, I was speechless and stymied, searching my mind for an apt saying. Slowly, I uttered a much-repeated proverb

---

3 Susie Hoogasian Villa, *100 Armenian Tales* (Detroit: Wayne State University Press, 1966), p. 36.

from my childhood: "Have intelligent enemies; don't have foolish friends." Since there was no relevance to the situation, this quote was left dangling. Proverbs are meant to hammer home an idea and bring meaning to the message; trying to induce a proverb usually draws a blank. So what may seem an easy method of collecting oral proverbs is far more complicated, and the mind of a purveyor is not always assured of a vault to draw on. Since these proverbs were recorded as they were heard, they may not conform to academic collections, where words may vary and nuances may change the message.

Keeping this in mind, in order to validate a proverb, it must be recorded instantly as it is heard, or it will be lost. Some examples follow.

At a lecture, a person coming down the aisle spotted an old friend. With a joyous smile on his face, he kiddingly but satirically said, "The goat's least savored weed grows under his nose." (A paradoxical way of saying "Happy to see you!")

Another time, at a family gathering, disrespect was shown to an elderly gentleman. In response, a guest said, "The donkey, which is a donkey, will bow its head when the church bell chimes." (Even a dumb animal knows respect.)

In another setting, a Genocide survivor, while in Turkey, sought out her husband's family and with great difficulty brought them to America. More gratitude was shown to her husband than to her for her courageous sacrifice. She quoted, "Raise the black crow, so it will gouge your eye out." (Lack of appreciation for the effort of the doer.)

While seated at an Armenian wake dinner, a son called from India. He was to give a wedding toast and needed a fitting proverb for the bride and groom. His mother suggested, "May you grow old on one pillow." (May you grow old together.)

On a luncheon date, a friend asked, "Does your daughter help you around the house?" The answer: "As a chicken does (nothing), the weeds sprout up everywhere." (Laziness results in nothing.)

At a church board meeting, a controversial issue arose, and contention began. Amid the clamor, a member said, "(He) caught a cold through the keyhole." (The situation was blown out of proportion.)

While aboard a French riverboat, an Armenian entertained the passengers between the many dinner courses. He was a born jokester, and the stories went on and on without stopping. Between laughs, he paused and said in Armenian, "My mother always said, 'Even if your jaw were to fall into the water, it wouldn't stop.'" (He was a nonstop talker.)

One more example. During the Watergate investigations in the 1970s, a discussion brought out an appropriate Armenian proverb: "The fish rots from the head." (Corruption starts from the top.)

And so these proverbs gave stronger context to the situation, effectively enhancing the thought.

After decades of collecting Armenian proverbs, the journey has ended. The era of the early-twentieth-century immigrants' oral influence has also passed, but their silenced voices will speak through the power of the printed word. There was a time to collect, a time to record, and now it is time to reap the proverbial harvest to reveal the wisdom of the Armenian soul.

After researching other collections, I decided that the proverbs needed some type of structure for identification. Many proverbs were diffused in my mind; I felt the wind had blown them hither and yon into disarray, demanding some form of order. As I studied these varied sayings, key words and thoughts kept popping up: God, good, father, mother, cat, dog, eye, ear, flowers, trees, and others. How to sort these words to make sense was problematic. So began the arduous task of aligning these terms under broad, relevant headings for easy subject access. The topics are as follows:

- Advice and Admonishment
- Body and Sensory
- Family
- God, Good and Evil
- Health
- Living Creatures
- Morality and Wisdom
- Nature
- People

Many proverbs fit into more than one category. For example, "The fish rotted from the head" has two key words: *fish* and *head*. The word *fish* would come under the topic of Living Creatures, and *head* would come under Body and Sensory. This seemed a workable solution to categorizing by key word.

Villagers were earthy, folksy, and plainspoken, and their proverbs were expressed in their colloquial language. Being aware of this, I found it necessary to bring attention to some of the irregular ones that needed to be clarified, or else they would make no sense. However, all are included, without censorship, because they reflect Armenian oral tradition. Examples follow.

> *Archaic*. "(My) daughter, I'll tell you. Daughter-in-law, you understand" (village of Garva/Sivas, Turkey). This reflects the patriarchal custom of very early oral tradition where the father-in-law never spoke directly to the son's new wife. Irrelevant today but invaluable in capturing the culture of the past.
>
> *Esoteric*. "Don't laugh like crazy Hovaness!" (village of Chanakhchee/Keghi, Turkey). Refers to a foolish villager.
>
> *Vulgar*. "His mind and brain are mixed with kaka!" (village of Kharpet, Turkey). Expresses a confused mind. "The dog's kaka doesn't stay under the snow" (village of Kharpet, Turkey). A graphic way to expose truth.
>
> *Prejudicial*. "When the dog's need comes, he dirties on the enemy's doorstep"(village of Agin, Turkey). Censorship does not deny the existence of prejudicial proverbs. It was decided to include them here, despite their unsavoriness, because these proverbs reflected the attitude of some villagers.
>
> *Armenian proverbs with Turkish words*. "When gold falls in mud it is still gold" (village of Everek/Caesarea, Turkey). The word for mud used in this proverb is *chamoor* and is Turkish.

Readers, be aware of unknown words in many of the Armenian proverbs; thus began my amateur attempt to identify them. With a Turkish dictionary in hand, the search began for some of these questionable word entries. Not surprisingly, since the Armenians were living among the Turks and the Kurds, Turkish words seeped into the Armenian vernacular and were entered as heard.

Here are a few common Turkish words used in many proverbs and everyday conversation:

- *Aman!* (ah! pity!)
- *Araba* (cart, wagon)
- *Aslan* (lion, courage)
- *Astar* (lining)
- *Ayaz* (cold)
- *Bent* (dam)
- *Chamoor* (mud)
- *Davul* (drum)
- *Deve* (camel)
- *Diri* (lively)
- *Domates* (tomato)
- *Esmer* (brown)
- *Haram* (forbidden)
- *Helal* (legitimate)
- *Huner* (skill)
- *Mal* (property)
- *Marifet* (art/knowledge)
- *Maskara* (ridiculous)
- *Mida* (stomach)
- *Orneg* (example)
- *Palan* (saddle)
- *Peskir* (hand towel)
- *Pirinc* (rice)
- *Pis* (dirty)
- *Sabun* (soap)
- *Sag(h)* (healthy)
- *Sakat* (crippled person)
- *Salata* (salad)
- *Sarma* (act of wrapping)
- *Sel* (flood)
- *Surat* (face)
- *Tas* (mug, saucer)
- *Tava* (pan)
- *Tempel* (lazy, idle, slow)
- *Tepe* (head)
- *Tepsi* (tray)
- *Ters* (contrary, inside out)
- *Topal* (lame)

One of my earlier Armenian translators mistakenly switched some of the Turkish words into proper Armenian, which was in error for the integrity of this collection. Later Armenian translators, aware of this substitution, entered the proverbs as heard. Regardless of some diversions, this collection reflects the Armenian culture.

Methodology

I never anticipated that collecting Armenian proverbs would be a serious undertaking before a chance meeting with my friend Susie Hoogasian Villa in the 1960s. At the time, she was working on the manuscript of her book *100 Armenian Tales*. While we shared memories of our common childhood background in Delray, I told her of my fun passion for collecting orally heard Armenian proverbs and lore. It was obvious that Susie's passion for the preservation of Armenian oral tradition was intense and purposeful, while my approach was just in pursuit of an enjoyable interest, a hobby—and a personally nostalgic one at that. With friendly earnestness, she urged me to collect and record with intention, for a purpose. Now this enjoyable pursuit became a mandate for preservation of Armenian oral tradition.

After that, I started a serious venture into collecting Armenian lore. What started out as an avocation in the 1950s now took root for a more poignant, significant purpose. Time was passing, and so were the informants, taking with them their precious repository of old-country oral tradition. The urgency to collect intensified. Susie's admonition and foresight brought this proverb collection to fruition. The 1960s through the 1980s produced my most prolific collection of orally heard and recorded proverbs and sayings.

Time does not stand still; it evolves. The time to listen and record proverbs is no longer available in the Delray Armenian-language community. Delray and its Armenian immigrant legend are history. However, the word of mouth of the villager has been captured in print, so the richness of Armenian lore will not be lost; it is in trust and protected.

Gradually, after many years of assimilating graciously into the Western culture, the threads of Armenian old-world customs have weakened in the diaspora. How can this tapestry, which is now fragile and loosely woven, become strengthened? One obvious answer would be gathering and preserving any orally expressed Armenian lore, which is the purpose of this collection. Also sustaining this binding thread have been the Armenian Church and the indomitable Armenian spirit of our immigrant parents; they left us a fragment of our inheritance through oral tradition, and our legacy is to perpetuate this meager thread through our progeny. Novelist Pat Conroy said it best: "When you put it on paper, it can never change."

For hundreds of years, Armenian proverbs have been communicated effectively. Now that tradition is fading. Why, then, is it of paramount concern to collect and protect orally heard Armenian proverbs now? There is an awareness today of the lack of documentation of proverbs on the endangered languages list, and, not surprising though sad, western Armenian is on that list.[4] In view of this awareness, there is a call for collecting and printing these endangered-language proverbs. The article also states that these proverbs are best preserved when collected from the informants' language community or in the appropriate immigrant area. Fortunately, this proverb collection was amassed as heard, by word of mouth, from immigrant informants at a prime time of availability; otherwise, the proverbs would have been lost. Hopefully, this collection answers the call.

Why is this Armenian collection important, and whom does it serve? This is a legitimate question and needs an answer. These proverbs help us understand the pulse of the Armenian villager; they tell us a story and reflect very early oral tradition. Amazingly, these proverbs reveal a whole new look at the vista of past Armenian village life. In my opinion, those served are folklorists, for comparative ethnic studies; Armenologists; the post-Genocide generation, linked to their parents; and future progeny, linked to ancestral lore.

This collection of proverbs has been in the making for half a century. The lessons each proverb teaches, the joy each brings, and the thoughts each provokes all came from an ancient culture rich in tradition, filled with love, and marred by great tragedy. Justly, these proverbs will not only have an impact for Armenians but will reach out to the lives of all who read them to teach, enlighten, guide, question, and entertain toward a deeper bond with and concern for our fellow man; we are more alike in our humanity than we are different. Reviewing other ethnic proverbs seems to prove that there is a universality among the contexts of proverbs.

In reviewing and comparing varied collections, I found many similar proverbs repeated for different ethnic groups. This leads me to believe that there is a universality in the context of word-of-mouth proverbs. Perhaps the dissemination of Erasmus's *Adagio* proverb collection throughout Europe was a factor that influenced this. It is important to note that despite dissimilar backgrounds, there is a common denominator binding these peoples: humanity, with its exigencies of life. Proverbs were used to expose, explain, and express them. A few pithy words were all that was needed.

Here are a few examples:

- *Arabic:* "The death of a friend is equivalent to the loss of a limb."

  Armenian: "The death of a husband is like a woman who loses her backbone."

[4] Talar Chahinian, "Western Armenian in Peril: UNESCO's Recognition and the Question of Contemporary Literature in the Exilic Language," *Asbarez*, August 4, 2010.

- *Chinese:* "To forget one's ancestors is to be a brook without a source, a tree without a root."
  Armenian: "A tree stands taller when it knows its roots."

- *Danish:* "He who is afraid to ask is ashamed of learning."
  Armenian: "It is not a shame to ask; it is a shame not to know."

- *English:* "He who falls in the sea will reach for foam."
  Armenian: "He who falls in the sea will reach for the foam.'

- *French:* "To know a man well, one must have eaten a bushel of salt with him."
  Armenian: "Until you eat a kilo of salt with your friend, you won't know who he is."

- *German:* "One has only to die to be praised."
  Armenian: "Go die, then I will love you."

- *Icelandic:* "Two are an army against one."
  Armenian: "(Among three people), when two mouths become one, they kaka on the third one."

- *Russian:* "Many a man has reared a crow that later hacked his eyes out."
  Armenian: "Raise the black crow, so it will gouge your eye out."

- *Spanish:* "He who spits above himself will have it fall in his face."
  Armenian: "Don't throw a stone up; it will fall on your head on its way down."

- *Yiddish:* "If it's born of a cat, it'll catch mice."
  Armenian: "A cat, which is a cat, will run after the mouse."

Though historical happenings almost annihilated this ancient people, they withstood wars, exiles, and genocides—and survived. William Saroyan said it best: "For when two of them meet anywhere in the world, see if they will not create a new Armenia." We in the Armenian diaspora have succeeded, and there is a strong pulse that keeps this spirit alive. The beat cannot be subdued, as it has manifested itself through different veins for survival, and one of these channels is the printed word.

So this proverb collection is important to Armenians and to our progeny. The fact that Armenian proverbs are still used in our language culture validates the importance of this collection.

You might ask why an octogenarian would want to tackle the daunting task of putting forth an Armenian proverb book. The explanation is easy and meaningful. We, the first generation born in America of Armenian parentage, were vital to the continued saga of the twentieth-century unrecognized Armenian Genocide, which obliterated much of the traditional lore. It is with this fervor that I write. How did this affect my generation? Oral history is the heartbeat of a culture; with the dwindling of our parents' generation, Armenian oral history needed to be recorded. My experiences as a marginal person, bridging the gap between the inherited culture of my parents and the assimilated culture of being born in America, lead me to retain a semblance of past Armenian ethos. Perhaps it is a little late, but I write with hope to sustain what I have collected since the 1950s. The purpose of this collection is to keep the Armenian culture alive. It is with a glimmer of hope that the written word will prevail for our children.

I hope that my presentation of Armenian proverbs and sayings will fulfill this mandate and give identity and value to our progeny. An Armenian proverb gives credence to acknowledging the past: "A tree stands taller when it knows its roots." Well-known Armenian artist Martiros Sarian captured the root of the Armenian spirit with these words: "The earth like a living thing has its own spirit, and without one's native land, without close touch with one's Motherland, it is impossible to find one's self, one's Soul."[5]

---

5 Shahen Khachaturian, *Sarian* (Yerevan: Martiros Sarian Museum, 2001), p. 7.

Photo Album

Looking Back at Old Delray through Photographs

Above: My wedding to Archie, family photo. Front row: My father, Herbert Kadian; me; my father-in-law, Haig Gopigian. Second row: My mother, Nevart (Doctorian) Kadian, and my mother-in-law, Dzaghig Gopigian. Third row: Hachig "Archie" Gopigian. The wedding was at St. John's Armenian Apostolic Church on Oakman Boulevard, Detroit. 1950. My mother, Nevart, and my mother-in-law, Dzaghig, were sources of many proverbs.

Left: My great-grandmother Mayrakhan Doctorian. My mother was raised by her grandmother Mayrakhan after the untimely death of her mother, Tacqouhi. Mayrakhan was my inspiration for folklore. Mayrakhan died from cholera in 1925 in Istanbul. Circa 1925.

My brothers and uncle posing on the occasion of George Kadian's high school graduation. From left: George Kadian, Uncle Charlie Kadian, Mike Kadian. Charlie Garabed Kadian was a young Armenian Genocide survivor who fled his captors by running down the mount in Shabinkraissar. 1948.

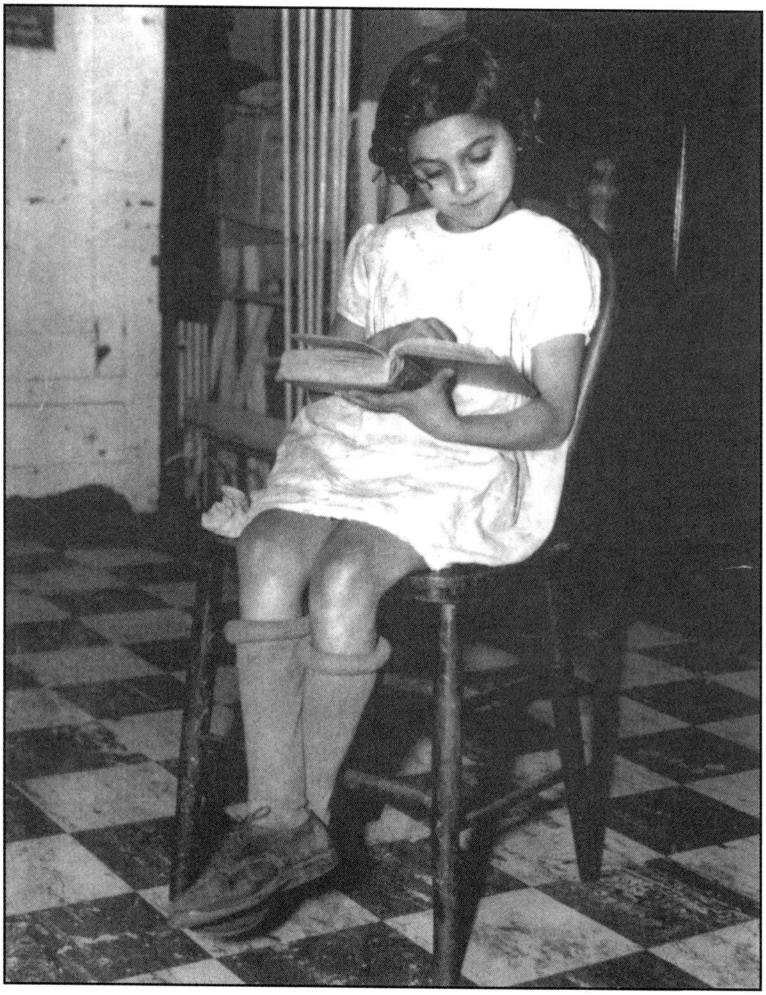

My friend Marian Engoian Fontichiaro at the Delray Community Center. Circa late 1930s. Courtesy of Marian Engoian Fontichiaro.

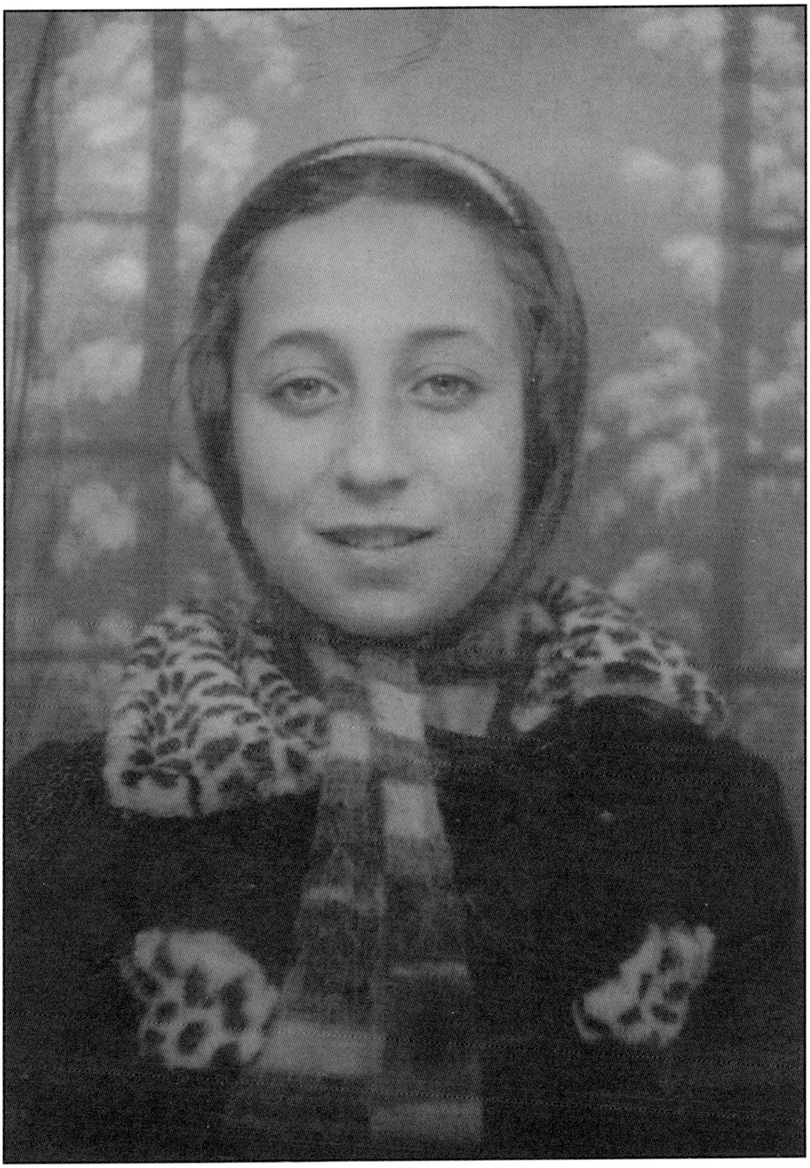

Me at age eight in my favorite leopard-collared coat. This beloved coat was purchased from Zuieback's during the Depression years. 1937.

Top left: Me standing beside my father, Herbert Kadian, and my soon-to-be husband, Archie Gopigian, at Edison Lake. 1949.

Top right: Typical family homes of Delray. 2012.

Family picnic at a local park. From left: Armenouhi Gopigian, unknown, Nevart Kadian, Dzaghig Gopigian. Circa 1940s.

Armenian proverb informants: Armen Mechigian, Susie Hoogasian Villa, Irene Baharozian, and Anahid Vart celebrating Archie Gopigian's fiftieth birthday with family friend Richard Megerian. 1976.

Susie Hoogasian Villa, my mentor and friend. She is the author of *100 Armenian Tales* (1966) and *Armenian Village Life before 1914* (1982). Early 1970s.

Alice Nigoghosian and John Villa at a book launch for *Armenian Village Life before 1914*, by Susie Hoogasian Villa, at the home of Michael and Emma Minasian in Bloomfield Hills, Michigan. The book was published posthumously by Wayne State University Press in 1982. Circa 1983.

Historic Fort Wayne at West Jefferson Avenue between South Crawford Street and South Livernois Avenue. This was the primary induction center for Michigan troops entering battle from the Civil War to Vietnam. During World War II, my friends and I could observe Italian prisoners of war from West Jefferson Avenue. Courtesy of Walter P. Reuther Library, Archives of Labor and Urban Affairs, Wayne State University. Date unknown.

Left: Delray Fire Station No. 29 on West Jefferson Avenue near Crossley. 2012. Top right: Peninsular Savings Bank and Post Office Building on West Jefferson Avenue near West End. 2002. Bottom right: Art Deco bank, West Jefferson Avenue. 1999. Although it is in a state of disrepair, this was an important landmark because many Armenians (including my mother, Nevart Kadian) banked there. It was one of the newer iconic buildings of the time. I remember being very sad upon hearing of the death of Will Rogers while I was in front of the building on August 15, 1935.

Top: Delray General Hospital at 7125 West Jefferson Avenue near Green Street. Many of my friends were born at this hospital. I was born at home around the corner on Green Street. Courtesy of Walter P. Reuther Library, Archives of Labor and Urban Affairs, Wayne State University. Circa 1960s.

Bottom: Detroit Police Station on Fort Street and Green. 2010.

Top: James McMillan Elementary School (first through eighth grades) on West End Street near South Street. I attended fourth grade at this school, and my brother Mike attended kindergarten. Susie Hoogasian Villa attended kindergarten through eighth grade. Courtesy of Walter P. Reuther Library, Archives of Labor and Urban Affairs, Wayne State University. Date unknown.

Left: James Campbell Branch of the Detroit Public Library on West Fort Street near Waterman. I frequented this beloved library, which also was a wonderful resource of Armenian books for my mother. The library was relocated to Vernor Highway and Cabot Street around 2006. Circa 2002.

Cary Elementary School on South and Crawford Streets. I graduated from this school with many of my Armenian friends in 1942. My brothers also attended this school. Courtesy of Walter P. Reuther Library, Archives of Labor and Urban Affairs, Wayne State University. Date unknown.

Cary Elementary School graduation. My classmates and I in 1942. I am third from right in the front row on the lawn of Cary School. 1942.

Two views of Southwestern High School at Waterman and Fort Streets. My brother George, dear friends Justina Zoanetti and Irene Ossian, and I graduated from this school. 2012.

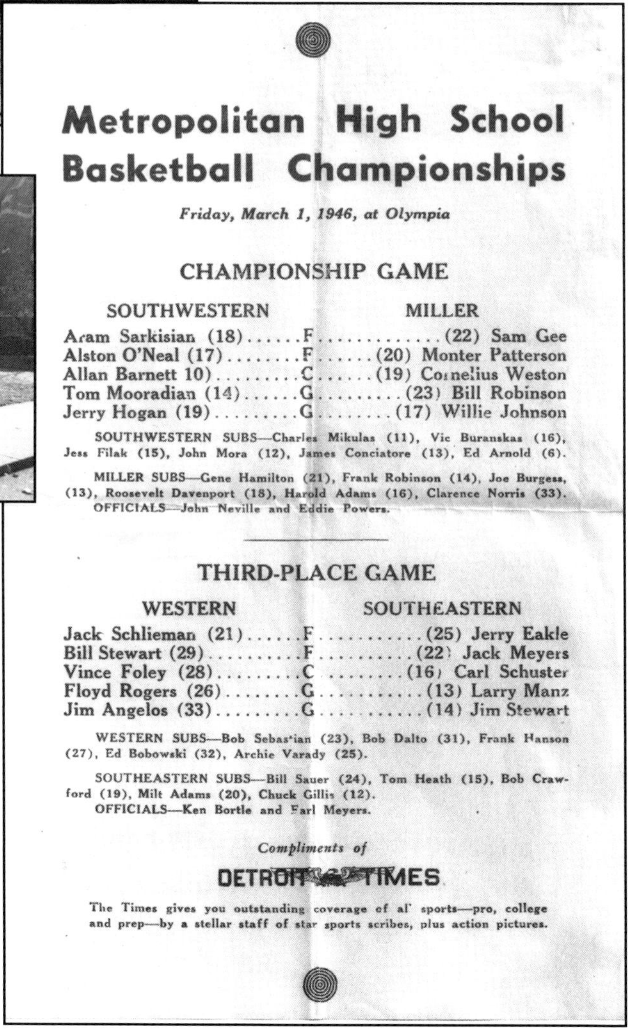

Metropolitan High School Basketball Championships

Friday, March 1, 1946, at Olympia

CHAMPIONSHIP GAME

SOUTHWESTERN		MILLER
Aram Sarkisian (18)	F	(22) Sam Gee
Alston O'Neal (17)	F	(20) Monter Patterson
Allan Barnett 10)	C	(19) Cornelius Weston
Tom Mooradian (14)	G	(23) Bill Robinson
Jerry Hogan (19)	G	(17) Willie Johnson

SOUTHWESTERN SUBS—Charles Mikulas (11), Vic Buranskas (16), Jess Filak (15), John Mora (12), James Conciatore (13), Ed Arnold (6).

MILLER SUBS—Gene Hamilton (21), Frank Robinson (14), Joe Burgess, (13), Roosevelt Davenport (18), Harold Adams (16), Clarence Norris (33).
OFFICIALS—John Neville and Eddie Powers.

THIRD-PLACE GAME

WESTERN		SOUTHEASTERN
Jack Schlieman (21)	F	(25) Jerry Eakle
Bill Stewart (29)	F	(22) Jack Meyers
Vince Foley (28)	C	(16) Carl Schuster
Floyd Rogers (26)	G	(13) Larry Manz
Jim Angelos (33)	G	(14) Jim Stewart

WESTERN SUBS—Bob Sebastian (23), Bob Dalto (31), Frank Hanson (27), Ed Bobowski (32), Archie Varady (25).

SOUTHEASTERN SUBS—Bill Sauer (24), Tom Heath (15), Bob Crawford (19), Milt Adams (20), Chuck Gillis (12).
OFFICIALS—Ken Bortle and Earl Meyers.

Compliments of

DETROIT TIMES

The Times gives you outstanding coverage of all sports—pro, college and prep—by a stellar staff of star sports scribes, plus action pictures.

Program of Metropolitan High School Basketball Championship Game at Olympia Stadium in 1946. Two Armenians (Tom Mooradian and Aram Sarkisian) were on the Southwestern team that won the state championship. The Delray Armenian community was very supportive of this team. *Detroit Times*, March 1, 1946.

Top: Armenian Cultural Center (Hye Getron). Also known as the Findlater, the ACC was located on West Lafayette Boulevard and Beard Street. It was purchased in 1941, and church services were provided at this location to serve the southwest Detroit Armenian community. This former Masonic temple included St. Sarkis Armenian Church on the second floor, along with Armenian-language classrooms and Armenian Relief Society facilities. The first floor included a large auditorium (also used as a banquet hall) and a stage. The third floor was a museum of the Armenian Revolutionary Federation with artifacts from the First Armenian Republic. The lower level included a kitchen, a small hall, a room for the Armenian Youth Federation (open nightly for recreation), and a coffee house (actually, a man cave). Despite the lack of adequate parking, this facility was utilized from the early 1940s through the early fall of 1962, until the consecration of the new St. Sarkis Armenian Church on October 14, 1962, in Dearborn. 2013. Special thanks to journalist Mitch Kehetian.

Zavarian Hall on Cottrell and Erie Streets was erected by Armenians in 1928. This multipurpose hall was an important social center for Delray Armenians. Before churches were built, this was where Armenian wedding ceremonies and receptions were held. The hall was also used for Armenian-language classes, dances, family *khunchooks*, and political meetings. It even had a men's gathering place for sharing Armenian coffee (*sourj*). It was sold in the 1950s because there were few Armenians left in Delray. From Dr. Ashod Rhaffi Aprahamian, *Remarkable Rebirth: The Early History of the Armenians in Detroit* (2005).

Holy Cross Hungarian Church at South and Yale Streets, serving the area's Hungarian residents. 2012.

All Saints Catholic Church at 7824 West Fort Street near West End Street, serving the area's Italian Catholic residents. The final mass there was held on December 31, 2017. 2012.

Top: Delray Community Center on Cottrell and Erie Streets (across from the Zavarian Hall). My brothers and I and many Armenian friends attended Sunday school here in the 1930s. The center offered many activities for youth, educational classes for homemakers, and a second floor for playing basketball. It was built and maintained by the largesse of the Presbyterian Church. 1999.

Right: St. John Cantius Catholic Church at 844 South Harbaugh and Dearborn Streets, serving the area's Polish residents. The final mass there was held on October 28, 2007. 2012.

Good Hope Lutheran Church on South and Post Streets, probably built by German immigrants. 2012.

Hollywood Theater at 4809 West Fort Street. As a child in the 1930s, I attended a live musical stage performance with my mother at this majestic theater built in 1927. In the 1940s and 1950s, this was a favorite venue for seeing hit Hollywood movies featuring notable stars of the time. In 1963, the building was razed, probably due to a lack of adapting to modern technology and an inconvenient location. Courtesy of the Burton Historical Collection, Detroit Public Library. 1930.

Lockeman's Hardware and Boats at 7630 West Jefferson Avenue (between South Solvay and South Crossley Streets). This hardware store catered to local families, businesses, and boaters. I was surprised to learn that at this date, it is still functioning. 2012.

Fancy Pastry Shop was opened at 8006 West Jefferson Avenue and later moved to 8148 West Jefferson (between South Cary and South Sloan Streets) by Hungarian immigrant Steve Lehoczky. It was at this location until the 1970s, when it moved to Allen Park. Currently, it is in its third generation, run by Steve's grandson Al Kocsisko. Many of my friends and I ordered the famous Hungarian torte cake for our weddings. Fancy Pastry Shop was well known and patronized by many of Detroit's high-end restaurants. The photo shows my high school friend Margaret Lehoczky behind the pastry counter. Circa 1934.

Window display of Hungarian torte cakes at the Fancy Pastry Shop. It was every Delray bride's dream to serve this special cake with buttercream frosting at her wedding. Circa 1934.

Photos courtesy of Margaret Lehoczky Kocsisko.

Hungarian children in costumes. Hungarians were noted for their fine embroidery. I remember grade-school Hungarian girlfriends Erane, Marishka, and Ilona wearing embroidered blouses. Courtesy of Walter P. Reuther Library, Archives of Labor and Urban Affairs, Wayne State University. Circa late 1930s, 1940s.

Below: Hungarian Village Club. This popular nightclub featured music by talented Hungarian Gypsy performers and delicious Hungarian food. Note the musicians' spat footwear, evoking a past era. Courtesy of Walter P. Reuther Library, Archives of Labor and Urban Affairs, Wayne State University. Circa 1930s.

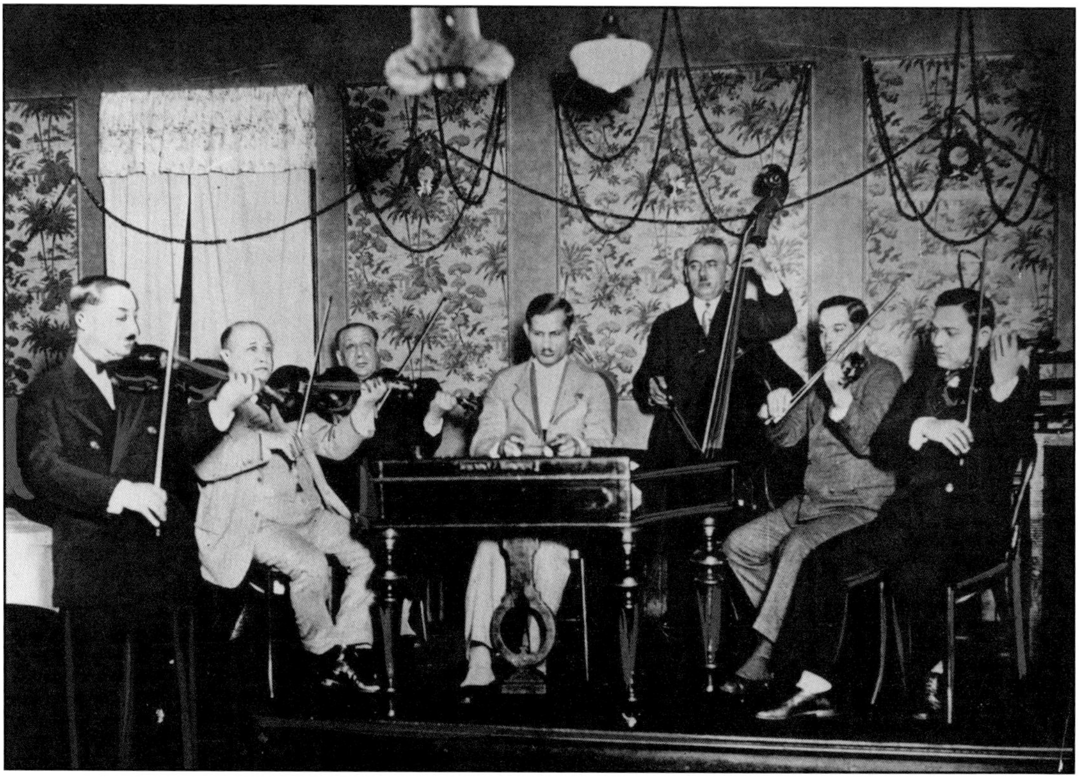

Delray (Hungarian) Theater on West Jefferson between Dearborn Street and West End Street, adjacent to the larger Grande Theater. Hungarian-language movies were shown here, and it was a favorite venue for Hungarian immigrants. Growing up with Hungarian friends, I understood some Hungarian and remember seeing an emotional Hungarian movie about a sick little girl who was healed. Courtesy of the Burton Historical Collection, Detroit Public Library. Circa 1940s.

Hungarian Village Club at 8160 West Jefferson at the corner of South Sloan Street. People were drawn to this popular nightclub from all over metro Detroit. It was a noted entertainment center with food, music, and dancing. Courtesy of Walter P. Reuther Library, Archives of Labor and Urban Affairs, Wayne State University. Circa 1940s.

Neisner Bros. Inc. 5 cent to $1.00 Store at West Jefferson and Dearborn Streets. This was the local variety store, part of a chain. This photo depicts a strike during the Christmas season. Note the fur-trimmed boots and seamed silk stockings worn by the women. Neisner was the hub of Delray, where friends met and where there was something for everyone. Courtesy of Walter P. Reuther Library, Archives of Labor and Urban Affairs, Wayne State University. Circa 1940s.

Opposite page, top: Detroit Produce Terminal (formerly Detroit Union Terminal) at 7201 West Fort and Green Streets. My father (see business card), Herbert Kadian, conducted his produce business through this terminal. At infrequent visits, I was always awed at the strength of my father swinging potato sacks from railroad box cars onto the platform. 2012.

Opposite page, bottom: Solvay Industrial Chemicals Detroit Plant on West Jefferson. This company made soda ash and provided jobs for many local men, including many Armenians. It paved the local roads and built the neighborhood's first hospital. Courtesy of Walter P. Reuther Library, Archives of Labor and Urban Affairs, Wayne State University. Circa 1950s. *Detroit Metro Times*, October 21, 2009.

H. KADIAN
Produce Distributor
547 South Livernois
Detroit, Mich.

ENTRANCE
ONLY

Armenian Proverbs
and
Expressions

In Memoriam

Hourig Toukhanian Jacobs

"...And when you work with love
you bind your self to yourself
and to one another,
and to God."

—Kahlil Gibran, *The Prophet*

Armenian Proverbs and Expressions

Collected in Armenian, Translated and Transliterated into English

Հարցնելը ամօթ չէ, չգիտնալը ամօթ է:

1

Advice and Admonishment

"Asking is not a shame, not knowing is a shame."

1 If I say chick, understand that I mean chick peas.
(If I give you a hint, get my meaning.)

Լէ ըսեմ, լէպլէպի հասկցիր։
Leh ushem, leblebee hasguhtseer.

2 Even if you know a thousand things, ask the person who knows only one.

Եթէ նոյնիսկ հազար բան գիտես մէկ բան գիտցողին հարցուր։
Yeteh nooyneesg hazar pan keedes, meg pan keedtsogheen hartsoor.

3 Asking is not a shame, not knowing is a shame.

Հարցնելը ամօթ չէ, չգիտնալը ամօթ է։
Hartsuhneluh amot cheh, chuhkeednaluh amot eh.

4 If the mountain does not suit you, you must adapt to the mountain.

Լեռը քեզի չի յարմարիր, դուն լերան պիտի յարմարիս։
Leruh kezee chee harmareer, toon leran beedee harmarees.

5 He who does not hear (understand) with his ear will hear (understand) with his back (stick).

Ան որ չի լսեր ականջով, կը լսէ կռնակով։
An vor chee luhser aganchov, gu luhseh grnagov.

6 Whatever we learn in the cradle remains with us until the grave.

Ինչ որ կը սորվինք օրօրոցին մէջ, մինչեւ գերեզման կը տեւէ։
Eench vor guh sorveenk ororotseen mech, meenchev kerezman guh deveh.

7 For those who know, it's worthy; for those who don't know, it has no value.

Գիտցողին արժանի, չգիտցողին համար արժէք չկայ։
Keedtsogheen arzhanee, chuhkeedtsogheen hamar arjek chuhga

8 If you have an intelligent son, why do you need money? If you have a foolish son, why do you need money?

Եթէ խելացի տղայ ունիս, դրամը ի՞նչ ընես, եթէ խենթ տղայ ունիս, դրամը ի՞նչ ընես։
Yeteh khelatsee duhgha oonees, tuhramuh eench uhnes? Yeteh khent duhgha oonees, tuhramuh eench uhnes?

9	You don't butt your head with a fool. (You can't reason with a fool.)	Խենթին հետ գլուխ չես դներ։ *Khenteen hed kuhlookh ches tuhner.*
10	Whatever you learn is a gold bracelet on your arm.	Ինչ որ սորվիս, ձեռքիդ վրայ ոսկի ապարանջան է։ *Eench vor sorvees, tserkeet vuhra vosgee abaranchan eh.*
11	A new broom sweeps clean.	Նոր աւելը մաքուր կ'աւլէ։ *Nor aveluh makoor gavleh.*
12	Don't step into the water unless you can see the bottom.	Ան ջուրը որուն տակը չես տեսներ, մէջը մի՛ մտներ։ *An chooruh voroon daguh ches desner, mechuh mee muhdner.*
13	Keep your door closed, so you won't catch your neighbor at thievery.	Դուռդ գոց պահէ, դրացիդ գող մի՛ բռներ։ *Tooruht kots baheh, tuhratseet kogh mee puhrner.*
14	If you don't have money, bury yourself. (Without money, you cannot succeed.)	Չունիս փող, մտիր հող։ *Choonees pogh, muhdeer hogh.*
15	Who talks much errs much.	Շատ խօսողը շատ կը սխալի։ *Shad khosoghuh shad guh suhkhalee.*
16	Blessed is the stick that brings justice.	Օրհնեալ է այն փայտը, որ արդարութիւն կը բերէ։ *Orhnyal eh ayn payduh, vor artarootyoon guh pereh.*
17	A crooked ruler cannot make a straight line.	Ծուռ քանակէն շիտակ գիծ չ'ելլեր։ *Dzoor kanaguen sheedag keedz cheller.*
18	Long life doesn't bring knowledge. The much-traveled one acquires knowledge.	Երկար ապրողը բան չի գիտեր, շատ պտըտողը բան գիտէ։ *Yergar abroghuh pan chee keeder, shad buduhdoghuh pan keedeh.*

19 Where the fire falls, there it burns. (Pain is felt when it affects you.)	Կրակը ինկած տեղը կ՚այրէ: *Guhraguh eengadz deghuh gayreh.*
20 Don't get out of your shoes. (Don't live beyond your means.)	Կօշիկէդ դուրս մի՛ ելլեր: *Gosheeguehd toors mee yeller.*
21 One who counts the garlic and onions cannot eat pig feet stew. (Being cheap doesn't allow for enjoyment.)	Սոխն ու սխտորը հաշուողը փաչա չի կրնար ուտել: *Sokhn oo sukhdor hashvoghuh pacha chee guhrnar oodel.*
22 The snake, which is a snake, measures the soil he eats. (One who is cheap measures everything. Or: Discernment, wise as a serpent.)	Օձը որ օձ է խնայողաբար հողը կ՚ուտէ: *Otsuh vor ots eh khuhnayoghapar hoghuh goodeh.*
23 In your affluent days live frugally, so that in frugal days you can live abundantly.	Առատ օրիդ նեղ ապրէ՛, որ նեղ օրիդ լայն ապրիս: *Arad oreet negh abreh, vor negh oreet layn abrees.*
24 Even the water and the silt from the stream are helpful to the ocean.	Գետին ջուրն ու տիղմն ալ ծովին օգուտ ունին: *Kedeen choorn oo deeghmn al dzoveen okood ooneen.*
25 He who is content with his lot is the world's happiest man.	Ով որ իր ունեցածէն գոհ է, աշխարհին երջանիկ մարդն է: *Ov vor eer oonetsadzen koh eh, ashkharheen yerchaneeg martn e.*
26 Don't stick your foot out of the quilt. (Don't live beyond your means.)	Ոտքդ վերմակէդ դուրս մի՛ հաներ: *Vodkuht vermaget toors mee haner.*
27 Stretch your feet to the length of your quilt, roll your quilt to the length of your feet. (Live according to your means.)	Ոտքդ վերմակիդ համեմատ երկարէ, վերմակդ ոտքիդ չափ ոլորէ: *Vodkuht vermagueet hamemad yergareh, vermaguht vodkeet chap voloreh*

28 When you have too much butter, you brush it on your buttocks.
(When you have too much, you become extravagant.)

Եթէ շատ կարագ ունենաս, ոռիդ կը քսես:
Yeteh shad garak oonenas, vohreet guh kuhses.

29 Until you see the water, don't remove your shoes.

Ջուրը չտեսած կօշիկդ մի՛ հաներ:
Chooruh chuhdesadz, gosheeguht mee haner.

30 The meat for you, the bone for me.
(You have full authority; I will sacrifice for you.)

Միսը քեզի, ոսկորը ինծի:
Meesuh kezee, vosgoruh eendzee.

31 A long-threaded needle doesn't denote talent.
(Don't judge by appearance.)

Երկար դերձանը հուներ չէ:
Yergar tertsanuh hooner cheh.

32 Don't fly too high.
(Do not be carried away with self-importance.)

Շատ վերէն մի՛ թռիր:
Shad veren mee tuhreer.

33 I finished sifting and I hung up my sieve.
(My task is accomplished.)

Մաղս մաղեր եմ, պատը կախեր եմ:
Maghuhs magher em, baduh gakher em.

34 The yoke is borne from the great one.
(The burden is the responsibility of the master.)

Լուծը մեծէն կը ծնի:
Loodzuh medzen guh dzuhnee.

35 With our money, we became fools.
(We didn't get our money's worth and suffered.)

Մեր դրամով մասխարա եղանք:
Mer tuhramov maskhara yeghank.

36 Much went, little stayed.
(The worst has passed.)

Շատը գնաց, քիչը մնաց:
Shaduh kuhnats, keechuh mehnats.

37 To those who know, it's lawful; to those who don't, it's forbidden.
(Those in the know benefit, while those who are not will suffer.)

Գիտցողին հելալ է, չգիտցողին հէրամ ըլլայ:
Keedtsogheen helal eh, chuhkeedtsogheen heram uhlla.

38 What you learn in childhood is carved into stone; what you learn in old age is carved into ice.

Պզտիկութեանդ սորվածը քարին վրայ կը փորագրուի, մեծահասակ ժամանակ սորվածդ՝ սառոյցի:
Buhzdeegootyanuht sorvadzuh kareen vrah guh porakruhvee; medzahasag zhamanag sorvadzuht sarooytsee.

39 You may be asleep, but your luck is awake.

Դուն քուն, բախտդ արթուն:
Toon koon, pakhtuht artoon.

40 As many things as you know, there is much more you need to learn.

Որչափ բան գիտես, դեռ շատ սորվելիք ունիս:
Vorchap pan keedes, ter shad sorveleek oonees.

41 One who lacks sensitivity digs the ditch for another, and the dirt falls on his head.
(He is insensitive to others and suffers the consequences.)

Զգացում չունեցողը ուրիշին հողը կը փորէ, ու հողը իր գլխուն կը թափի:
Uhzkatsoom choonetsoghuh ooreesheen hoghuh guh poreh, oo hoghuh eer kuhlkhoon guh tapee.

42 Where bread, there tread.
(Go where you can earn a living.)

Ուր հաց, հոն կաց:
Oor hahts, hohn gahts.

43 A rolling stone holds no moss.
(No roots.)

Գլորուող քարը մամուռ չի բռներ:
Kuhlorvogh karuh mamoor chee puhrner.

44 Incense and candle find their path.
(Habits don't change.)

Խունկն ու մոմը կը գտնեն իրենց ճամբան:
Khoongn oo momuh guh kuhdnen eerents jampan.

45 My bread has no salt.
(I get no appreciation.)

Հացս աղ չունի::
Hatsuhs agh choonee.

46 By the time the intelligent one thinks it through, the fool crosses the bridge.

Մինչեւ խելացին մտածէ, խենթը կամուրջը կ'անցնի:
Meenchev khelatseen muhdadzeh, khentuh gamoorchuh gantsnee.

47 He drowned in his own spit.
(Much ado about nothing.)

Թուքին մէջ խեղդուեցաւ:
Tookeen mech kheghtuhvetsav.

48 Measure ten times, cut once.

Տասը չափէ, մէկ կտրէ:
Dasuh chapeh, meg guhdreh.

49 When your kaka comes, remain seated in your place.
(Hasty decisions lead to regret.)

Քաքդ գայ, տեղդ նստիր:
Kakuht kah, deghuht nuhsdeer.

50 You cannot set out (on the road) with another person's word.
(You cannot rely on other people's advice.)

Ուրիշին խօսքով ճամբայ չես կրնար ելլել:
Ooreesheen khoskov jampah ches guhrnar yellel.

51 Do for me, learn for yourself.

Ինծի համար ըրէ, քեզի համար սորվէ:
Eendzee hamar uhreh, kezee hamar sorveh.

52 Don't throw a stone up; it will fall on your head on its way down.

Դուն մի՛ նետեր վեր քար, դարձին կ'իյնայ գլխուդ վար:
Toon mee neder ver kar, tartseen geeynah kuhlkhoot var.

53 Thick and thin are the same price; woe to the one who spins thin.
(Woe to the one who is wasteful.)

Հաստն ու բարակը միեւնոյն գինն են, վա՜յն եկեր է բարակը մանողին:
Hasdn oo paraguh meeyevnooyn keenn en. Vayn yeger eh parag manogheen.

54 What isn't done today will not be done in a year.

Այսօրուան չեղածը տարիէն չ'ըլլար:
Aysorvan cheghadzuh dareeyen chuhllar.

55 Don't leave today's work until tomorrow.

Այսօրուան գործը վաղուան մի՛ ձգեր:
Aysorvan kordzuh vaghvan mee tsuhker.

56 The food that comes from others is not a meal, and it's not on time.

Ուրիշէն եկածը ժում չ'ըլլար, ան ալ ժամանակին չ'ըլլար:
Ooreeshen yegadzuh zhoom chuhllar, an al zhamanageen chuhllar.

57 I wish the least of the Armenian brain belonged to me.
(Turkish quote.)

Հայերուն վերջին խելքն իմս ըլլար:
Hayeroon vercheen khelkuh eemuhs uhllar.

58	If you spit up, it's your forehead. If you spit down, it's your beard. (You can't win.)	Վեր թքնես առիքդ է, վար թքնես մօրուքդ է: *Ver tuhknes areekuht eh, var tuhknes morookuht eh.*
59	Respect to be respected.	Յարգէ՛ որ յարգուիս: *Harkeh vor harkuhvees.*
60	Without the old, you can't have the new.	Երբ հինը չունիս, նորն ալ չես ունենար: *Yerp heenuh choonees, norn al ches oonenar.*
61	(He) caught a cold through the keyhole. (Exaggerated reaction.)	Բանալիին ծակէն պաղ բռնեց: *Panaleeyeen dzagen bagh puhrnetz.*
62	If you don't know where you're coming from, you won't know where you're going.	Եթէ չես գիտեր թէ ուրտեղէ՞ն եկած ես, չես գիտեր թէ ո՞ւրկ'երթաս: *Yeteh ches keeder teh oordeghen yegadz es, ches keeder oor gertas.*
63	Say it once, listen a thousand times.	Մէ'կ խօսք ըսէ, հազար լսէ: *Meg khosk uhseh, hazar luhseh.*
64	The dress that is not worn wears out.	Հագուստը՝ որ չէ հագուած, կը մաշի: *Hakoosduh, vor cheh hakvadz, guh mashee.*
65	Ask advice here and there, but you yourself decide.	Խորհուրդ հարցուր աստին-անդին, բայց ինքդ որոշէ: *Khorhoort hartsoor asteen-anteen, payts eenkuht vorosheh.*
66	Every round thing is not an apple.	Ամէն կլոր բան խնձոր չէ: *Amen guhlor pan khuntsor cheh.*
67	First think, then speak.	Առաջ մտածէ՛, յետոյ խօսէ՛: *Arach muhdadzeh, hedoh khoseh.*
68	Not every road leads to Rome.	Ամէն ճամբայ Հռոմ չի տանիր: *Amen jampah Huhrom chee daneer.*

69 Don't look above yourself, always look beneath you. (Be grateful for your situation.)	Քեզմէ վերը մի՛ նայիր, քեզմէ վարը նայիր: *Kezmeh veruh mee nayeer, kezmeh varuh nayeer.*
70 This thing is not gossip, this thing is fact.	Բամբասանք չէ, բանն ասանկ է: *Pampassank che, pann asang eh.*
71 Buying is not the skill, maintaining is the skill.	Առնելը մէրիֆէթ չէ, պահելը մէրիֆէթ է: *Arneluh merifet cheh, baheluh merifet eh.*
72 The outside (external) fire doesn't burn you, the inside (internal) fire burns you.	Դուրսի կրակը քեզ չի վառեր, ներսի կրակը կը վառէ: *Toorsee guhraguh kez chee varer, nersee guhraguh guh vareh.*
73 Every lid has a noise. (Everyone has an opinion.)	Ամէն ղափախ ձայն ունի: *Amen ghapakh tsayn oonee.*
74 One who enters the bath must perspire.	Բաղնիքը մտնողը պիտի քրտնի: *Paghneekuh muhdnoghuh beedee kuhrduhnee.*
75 What goes up must come down.	Ինչ որ վեր կ'երթայ, վար պիտի գայ: *Eench vor ver gertah, var beedee kah.*
76 Listen to elderly advice, so adversity won't touch you.	Մտիկ ըրէ մեծի խրատ, որ չհասնի փորձանք վրադ: *Mudeeg uhreh medzee khuhrad, vor chuhasnee portsank vuhraht.*
77 Where bread, there homeland.	Ուր հաց, հոն հայրենիք: *Oor hats, hon hayreneek.*
78 One who hurries doesn't arrive sooner.	Աճապարողը շուտ տեղ չի հասնիր: *Ajabaroghuh shood degh chee hasneer.*
79 Instead of the name, let the eye be cast out. (Reputation is more important.)	Անունը ելլելուն, աչքը թող ելլէ: *Anoonuh yelleloon, achkuh togh yelleh.*

80 One who enters the dance must shake his buttocks.
(Commitment involves participation. Roll with the punches.)

Պարի մտնողը ոոը պիտի շարժէ:
Baree mudnoghuh voruh beedee sharzheh.

81 Beat the iron while it's hot.
(Timing is paramount.)

Երկաթը տաք-տաք կը ծեծեն:
Yergatuh dahk-dahk guh dzedzen.

82 Give little, give heartily.

Քի՛չ տուր, սրտա՛նց տուր:
Keech door, suhrdantz door.

83 Walk narrowly during wide (ample) days, so you can walk widely during your narrow (lean) days.
(In your affluent days live narrowly, so in your narrow days you can live abundantly.)

Նեղ քալէ՛ քու լայն օրիդ, որ լայն քալես քու նեղ օրիդ:
Negh kaleh koo layn oreet, vor layn kales koo negh oreet.

84 Better late than not at all.

Լաւ է ուշ քան երբեք:
Lav eh oosh kan yerpek.

85 Don't hate, so you won't be hated.

Մի՛ ատեր, որ չատուիս:
Mee ader, vor chadvees.

86 Do good, cast it in the water; it will return and find you.

Բարիք ըրէ՛, ջո՛ւրը նետէ, անիկա կու գայ քեզի կը գտնէ:
Pareek uhreh, chooruh nedeh; aneegah goo kah kezee guh kuhdneh.

87 He builds castles in the air.
(He is delusional.)

Օդին մէջ դղեակներ կը շինէ:
Oteen mech tughyagner guh sheeneh.

88 Tie it short.
(Don't be long-winded.)

Կարճ կապէ:
Garj gabeh.

89 Puts water in the mortar and beats it.
(Inappropriate use.)

Ջուրը հրսանդին մէջ դրած կը ծեծէ:
Chooruh huhrsanteen mech tuhradz guh dzedzeh.

90 Luck runs ahead of him.
(Fortunate.)

Բախտը առջեւէն կը վազէ:
Pakhduh archeven guh vazeh.

91	He reads lolo to me. (He is fabricating stories.)	Ինծի լօլօ կը կարդայ: *Eendzee lolo guh gartah.*
92	May the writer (the angel of death) take him.	Գրողը տանի: *Kroghuh danee.*
93	Don't drop your sugar in the water. (Don't waste.)	Շաքարդ ջուրը մի՛ ձգեր: *Shakaruht chooruh mee tsuhker.*
94	Take one, hit it against the other. (Both are worthless.)	Մէկը առ միւսին զարկ: *Meguh ar, myoosseen zarg.*
95	The more you peel the onion, the more it can be peeled. (Endless gossip.)	Սոխը որքան կեղուես, կը կեղուուի: *Sokhuh vorchap geghves, guh geghvuhvee.*
96	There isn't anything harder than soil. (Problems need to be worked to produce results.)	Հողէն դժուարը չի կայ: *Hoghen tuhzhvaruh chee gah.*
97	Nothing is as cheap as the most expensive.	Սուղէն աժանը չի կայ: *Sooghen azhanuh chee gah.*
98	Eat and be satisfied.	Կե՛ր եւ գոհացիր: *Ger yev kohatseer.*
99	Come late, come sweet. (Your presence is always welcome.)	Ուշ եկուր, անուշ եկուր: *Oosh yegoor, anoosh yegoor.*
100	The spoken word flies, the written word remains.	Խօսքը կը թռի, գիրը կը մնայ: *Khoskuh guh tuhree, keeruh guh muhnah.*
101	Judgment came from your own mouth.	Ի բերնէ քումմէ դատուեցար: *Ee perneh koommeh tadvetsar.*
102	Look at the quality, not the quantity.	Քանակին մի՛ նայիր, որակին նայիր: *Kanageen mee nayeer, vorageen nayeer.*
103	Doesn't see the beam in his eye, sees the sliver in the eyes of others.	Իր աչքին գերանը չի տեսներ, ուրիշին աչքին շիւղը կը տեսնէ: *Eer achkeen keranuh chee desner, ooreesheen achkeen shyooghuh guh desneh.*

104 Who stands up in anger sits with harm. (The quick-tempered will suffer the consequences.)

Բարկութեամբ ոտքի ելլողը վնասով կը նստի:
Pargootyamp vodkee yelloghuh vuhnasov guh nuhsdee.

105 Don't judge, so you won't be judged.

Մի՛ դատեր, որ չդատուիս:
Mee tader, vor chuhtadvees.

106 It's better to have intelligent enemies than foolish friends.

Աւելի լաւ է խելացի թշնամի ունենալ, քան թէ անխելք բարեկամ:
Avelee lav eh khelatsee tuhshnamee oonenal, kan teh ankhelk paregam.

107 It's easy to be generous with other people's money.

Դիւրին է ուրիշին դրամով առատ ըլլալ:
Tyooreen eh ooreesheen tuhramov arad uhllal.

108 Think carefully before you take your next step.

Լաւ մը խորհէ՛, յետոյ յաջորդ քայլդ ա՛ռ:
Lav muh khorheh, hedoh hachort kayluht ar.

109 What you see (know), act like you didn't see (know).

Տեսածդ չտեսածի տեղ դի՛ր:
Desadzuht chuhdesadzee degh teer.

110 Believe only what your eyes see, only what your ears hear.

Աչքովդ տեսածին ու ականջովդ լսածին միայն հաւատա՛:
Achkovuht desadzeen oo aganchovuht luhsadzeen meeayn havadah.

111 Instead of opening your mouth, open your eyes. (Be aware.)

Բերանդ բանալու տեղ աչքդ բա՛ց:
Peranuht panaloo degh, achkuht pats.

112 Better to lose your eye than your name (reputation).

Աւելի լաւ է աչքդ կորսնցնես քան թէ անունդ:
Avelee lav eh achkuht gorsuhntsuhnes, kan teh anoonuht.

113 Let what I say be an earring on your ear; don't forget it.

Ասի ականջիդ օղ ըլլայ, մի՛ մոռնար:
Asee agancheet ogh uhllah; mee mornar.

114 Better not to have a head than to have a blackened forehead.
(Better not to lose your honor.)

Լաւ է գլուխ չունենալ, քան թէ սեւցած ճակատ մը ունենալ:
Lav eh kuhlookh choonenal, kan teh sevtsadz jagad muh oonenal.

115 Clench your teeth.
(Persevere.)

Ակռաղ սեղմէ՛:
Agrat seghmeh.

116 I say *pahn* (thing), you say *tahn* (yogurt drink).
(We don't communicate.)

Ես բան կ'ըսեմ, դուն թան կ'ըսես:
Yes pan guhsem, toon tan guhses.

117 Hang a blue bead to avoid the evil eye.
(A superstitious belief that the blue bead protects from evil.)

Կապոյտ ուլունք կախէ՛, որ աչքի չի գայ:
Gabooyd ooloonk gakheh, vor achkeeh chee kah.

118 Don't hang an ear.
(Don't heed.)

Ականջ մի՛ կախեր:
Aganch mee gakher.

119 Don't give face.
(Don't spoil, don't encourage.)

Երես մի՛ տար:
Yeres mee dahr.

120 Close one eye and one ear.
(Be forgiving.)

Մէկ աչքդ, մէկ ականջդ գոցէ՛:
Meg achkuht, meg aganchuht kotseh.

121 Instead of a finger measure of a father, have a thimble full of a mother.
(A mother can do more with less.)

Փոխանակ մատի չափ հայր ունենալու՝ մատնոցի չափ մայր ունեցիր:
Pokhanag madee chap hayr oonenaloo, madnotsee chap mayr oonetseer.

122 When buying cloth, look at the selvage; when marrying a girl, look at the mother.
(The daughter is what the mother is.)

Պասմա առնես եզերքը նայէ՛, աղջիկ առնես մօրը նայէ՛:
Basmah arnes, yezerkuh nayeh,; aghcheeg arnes, moruh nayeh.

123 Don't be fooled by a woman's beauty; rather, let her character be beautiful.

Կնոջ մը գեղեցկութեան մի՛ խաբուիր, թո՛ղ բնութիւնը գեղեցիկ ըլլայ:
Guhnoch muh keghetsgootyan mee khapveer; togh puhnootyoonuh keghetseeg uhllah.

124 (My) daughter, I'll tell you; daughter-in-law, you understand.
(The father speaks through the daughter to the daughter-in-law.)

Աղջիկս քեզի ըսեմ, հարս դո՛ւն հասկցիր։
Aghcheeguhs, kezee uhsem, hars toon hasguhtseer.

125 When you have a bad tooth, pull it out and be free. When you have a bad neighbor, pull away, move, and be free.

Գէշ ակռայ եթէ ունիս, քաշէ՛, հանէ՛, ազատի՛ր։ Գէշ դրացի եթէ ունիս, քաշուէ՛, գնա՛, ազատի՛ր։
Kesh agrah yeteh oonees, kasheh haneh, azadeer. Kesh tuhratsee yeteh oonees kashveh kuhnah, azadeer.

126 When you send a child for water, spank him first, then send him; after the cup is broken, it's no use.

Երեխան երբ ջուրը ղրկես, նախ ծեծէ՛, վերջը ղրկէ՛. գաւաթը կոտրելէն վերջ բան չ՚արժեր։
Yerekhan yerp chooree ghuhrges, nakh dzedzeh, verchuh ghuhrgeh; godrelen verch pan charzher.

127 Beat your wife, you will have beaten seven devils.
(Village superstition; removes evil from wife.)

Ծեծէ՛ կինդ, եօթը սատանայ ծեծած կ՚ըլլաս։
Dzedzeh geenuht, yotuh sadana dzedzadz guhllas.

128 Pay much attention to the evil talk.
(Be aware.)

Գէշ խօսք շատ մտիկ ըրէ։
Kesh khosk shad muhdeeg uhreh.

129 You must think good and throw the bad behind you.

Լաւը պիտի խորհիս, գէշը ետեւդ նետես։
Lavuh beedee khorhees, keshuh yedevuht nedes.

130 Don't drop pearls in front of swine.

Խոզերուն առջեւ մարգարիտ մի՛ նետեր։
Khozeroon archev markareed mee neder.

131 Whatever you plant, that's what you will reap.

Ինչ որ ցանես, այն կը հնձես։
Eench vor tsanes, ayn guh huhntses.

132 When you get old, you will understand and respect the aged.

Երբ ծերանաս՝ ծերին յարգը կ'իմանաս։
Yerp dzeranas, dzereen harkuh geemanas.

133 By what measure you weigh, the same measure will be dealt to you.

Ինչ չափով որ կը կշռես, նոյն չափով կը կշռուիս։
Eench chapov vor guhshres, nooyn chapov guh guhshruhvees.

134 As much as you stir, the smell will increase.
(Gossip breeds evil.)

Որչափ խառնես՝ հոտը կ'ելլէ։
Vorchap kharnes, hoduh gelleh.

135 Whatever I say, write it on ice.
(What I say is meaningless.)

Ինչ որ ըսեմ, սառին վրայ գրէ։
Eench vor uhsem, sareen vrah kuhreh.

136 Don't love too much, there is hate; don't hate too much, there is love.

Շատ մի՛ սիրեր, ատել կայ, շատ մի՛ ատեր, սիրել կայ։
Shad mee seerer, adel gah; shahd mee ader, seerel gah.

137 Whatever you holler into the well echoes back to you.
(You reap what you sow.)

Հորին մէջ ինչ որ պոռաս՝ ան կ'իմանաս։
Horeen mech eench vor boras, an geemanas.

138 When alive if you haven't done, when dead you will never do.
(Do good when alive.)

Ողջ մնաս չես ըրած, մեռնիս նէ հեչ չես ըրած։
Voghch uhllas ches uhrahdz, mernees neh hech ches uhradz.

139 Elevate yourself, elevate others.

Բարձրացի՛ր, բարձրացո՛ւր։
Partsratseer, partsratsoor.

140 Beware of jealousy, because jealousy will bite you first.

Զգուշացի՛ր նախանձէ, որովհետեւ նախ քեզի կը խածնէ։
Uhzkooshatseer nakhantseh, vorovhedev nakh kezee guh khadzneh.

141 Wash the feet, drink the water.
(Gratitude; thankfulness with humility.)

Ոտքը լուա՛, ջո՛ւրը խմէ։
Vodkuh luhvah, chooruh khuhmeh.

142 Good apples placed next to rotten ones will spoil, too.

Հոտած խնձորին քով լաւն ալ դնես, ան ալ կը հոտի։
Hodadz khuhntsoreen kov lavn al tuhnes, an al guh hodee.

143 When you see the Kurd, ask him for bread, so he won't ask you for bread. (Preempt him.)

Քիւրտը տեսնես, հաց ուզէ՛, որ քիւրտը քեզմէ հաց չուզէ։
Kyurduh desnes, hats oozeh, vor Kyurduh kezmeh hats choozeh.

144 As many languages as you know, that's how many persons you are.

Որքան լեզու գիտես՝ այնքան մարդ ես։
Vorkan lezoo keedes aynkan mart es.

145 Find the new, then throw away the old.

Նորը գտի՛ր, ետքը հինը նետէ։
Noruh kuhdeer, yedken heenuh nedeh.

146 One who digs another's well falls in himself.

Ուրիշին հոր փորողը ինքը մէջը կ'իյնայ։
Ooreesheen hor poroghuh eenkuh mechuh geeynah.

147 Don't eat (abuse) the rights of others.

Ուրիշին իրաւունքը մի՛ ուտեր։
Ooreesheen eeravoonkuh mee ooder.

148 If you like the rose, you must also like the thorn.

Վարդը սիրես, փուշն ալ պիտի սիրես։
Vartuh seeres, pooshn al beedee seeres.

149 Don't laugh like crazy John. (Don't be silly. Listen. Esoteric saying.)

Խենթ Յովհաննէսին պէս մի՛ խնդար։
Khent Hovhannesseen bes mee khuhntar.

150 Don't send an old man for a donkey or a young man for a bride. (Be aware of foolish behavior.)

Ծեր մարդ մի՛ ղրկեր էշի համար, երիտասարդ մի՛ ղրկեր հարսի համար։
Dzer mart mee ghuhrger eshee hamar, yereedasart mee ghuhrger harsee hamar.

151 The old enemy can't be a friend.

Հին թշնամին բարեկամ չ'ըլլար։
Heen tuhshnameen paregam chuhllar.

152 Wish well for your neighbor, so goodness will come to your head.

Բարի ուզէ դրացիիդ համար, որ բարի գայ գլխուդ:

Paree oozeh tuhratseeyeet hamar, vor paree kah klkhoot.

153 Eat with your friend, but do not do business with him.

Բարեկամիդ հետ հաց կե՛ր, բայց առեւտուր մի՛ ըներ:

Paregameet hed hats ger, payts arevdoor mee uhner.

154 The trash should be planted in the garden.
(Make use of everything; bury the bad; be frugal.)

Աղբը պարտէզը պիտի ցանես:

Aghbuh bardezuh beedee tsanes.

155 Until you eat a kilo of salt with your friend, you won't know who he is.
(Many experiences test a friend.)

Մինչեւ որ քիլօ մը աղ չուտես բարեկամիդ հետ, չես գիտեր թէ ով է:

Meenchev vor kilo muh agh choodes paregameet hed, ches keeder teh ov eh.

156 It is more acceptable to have an intelligent enemy than to have an ignorant friend.

Աւելի նախընտրելի է խելացի թշնամի ունենալ, քան թէ տգէտ բարեկամ:

Avelee nakhuhndrelee eh khelatsee tuhshnamee oonenal, kan teh duhked paregam.

157 Tell me who your friend is, and I'll tell you who you are.

Ըսէ ինծի բարեկամդ ով է, ըսեմ քեզի թէ դուն ով ես:

Uhseh eendzee paregamuht ov eh, uhsem kezee teh toon ov es.

158 All who laugh in your face are not your friends.

Ամէն երեսիդ խնդացողը բարեկամդ չէ:

Amen yereseet khuhntatsoghuh paregamuht cheh.

159 Don't be afraid of the obvious enemy, be afraid of the secret one.

Յայտնի թշնամիէն մի՛ վախնար, գաղտնի թշնամիէն վախցիր:

Haydnee tuhshnameeyen mee vakhnar, kaghdnee tuhshnameeyen vakhtseer.

160	If you give the dough to the baker, he will bake it right. (Seek an expert.)	Հացը հացագործին եթէ տաս շիտակ կ'եփէ։ *Hatsuh hatsakordzeen yeteh das sheedag gepeh.*
161	Take flour to a baker and you're still ahead, even if he takes half. (Being cheap sometimes costs more.)	Ալիւրը հացագործին տո՛ւր, շահաւոր կ'ըլլաս, եթէ նոյնիսկ կէսը առնէ։ *Alyooruh hatsakordzeen door, shahavor guhllas, yeteh nooyneesg gesuh arneh.*
162	To those who love you, be a servant; to those who don't, be a master. (Serve those who care.)	Քեզ սիրողին ծառայ եղիր, չսիրողին աղա եղիր։ *Kez seerogheen dzarah yegheer, chuhseerogheen aghah yegheer.*
163	With ownership you become a slave (to your things).	Մալովդ մալամըդ կ'ըլլաս։ *Malovuht malamuht guhllas.*
164	Go die, come (back), then I will love you. (Unappreciated while alive.)	Գնա՛ մեռիր, եկո՛ւր սիրեմ։ *Kuhnah mereer, yegoor seerem.*
165	Look for your enemy under your pillow. (The enemy can come from within.)	Թշնամիդ բարձին տակը փնտռէ։ *Tuhshnameet partseen daguh puhndreh.*
166	Throw it to God. (Trust Him.)	Աստուածին (Աստուծոյ) նետէ։ Asdvadzeen (Asdoodzo) nehdeh.
167	I say A, you understand B. (Understand my meaning.)	Ես Այբ կ'ըսեմ, դուն Բեն հասկցիր։ *Yes Ayp guhssem, toon Pen hasguhtseer.*
168	Word tie. (Word given; promise to marry.)	Խօսքկապ։ *Khoskgahb.*
169	May he grow up with mother and father. (A baptismal blessing.)	Հօրով մօրով մեծնայ։ *Horov morov medzna.*
170	The past is forgotten. (The past is to be forgotten.)	Անցուկը մոռցուկ է։ *Antsooguh mortsoog eh.*
171	Don't fall into the hands of a lawyer or a doctor.	Փաստաբան եւ բժիշկի ձեռքը չիյնաս։ *Pasdapahn yev pejeeshguee tserk cheeynahs.*

Advice and Admonishment

172 If you speak, you are bad; if you don't, you are a jackass.
(Speak the truth, and you are reviled; if you don't, you are a jackass.)

Խօսիս նէ գէշ կ'ըլլաս, չխօսիս նէ էշ կ'ըլլաս:
Khosseess ne kesh guhllahs, chkhosseess ne esh guellahs.

173 Talk about a good man, and he appears (out of nowhere).

Լաւ մարդը իր խօսքին վրայ կու գայ:
Lahv mahrtuh eer khoskeen vrah gooka.

174 Once the nightingale leaves the cage, he will not return.
(Lost opportunity.)

Պուլպուլը եթէ վանդակէն փախի, ետ չի վերադառնար:
Boolbooluh yeteh vantaguen pakhee, yed chee veratarnar.

175 His mind and brain are mixed with kaka.
(He is crazy, confused.)

Միտքը խելքը քաքին հետ խառնուած է:
Mitkuh, khelkuh kahkeen hed kharnevadz eh.

176 From where to where?
(Amazement. How did this happen?)

Ուր տեղէն ուր:
Oor deghen oor.

177 Keep your heart ample.
(Don't let things bother you.)

Սիրտդ լայն պահէ:
Seerduht layn baheh.

178 From mouth to mouth a mote becomes a log.
(Gossip, exaggeration.)

Բերնէ բերան՝ կ'ըլլայ գերան:
Perneh perahn, guhlla kerahn.

179 Good overcomes the bad.

Բարին չարը կը տանի:
Pareen charuh guh dahnee.

180 He talks to the walls.
(Nobody is listening.)

Պատերուն հետ կը խօսի:
Bahderoon hehd guh khossee.

181 I say, I hear.
(My advice is not heeded.)

Ես կ'ըսեմ՝ ես կը լսեմ:
Yes guhssem, yes guh luhssem.

182 When afflicted with stress (fright, terror), it affects the weakest part of the body.

Սոսկումը ունենաս, նազիկ տեղը կը բռնէ:
Sosgoomuh oonenahs, nahzeeg deghuh guh prneh.

183 He who gossips in front of you will also gossip behind you.

Առջեւդ խօսողը՝ ետեւդ ալ կը խօսի:
Archevuht khossoghuh, yedevuht ahl guh khossee.

184 Be wise, but let them think you're crazy.

Գիտնական եղիր, բայց թող խենթ կարծեն:
Keednagan yegheer, payts togh khent gardzen.

185 Say yes, go.
(Let it go; don't react.)

Հա՛ ըսէ, գնա՛:
Ha uhsseh, kena.

186 Every mother-in-law must put her son-in-law on her head.
(Let every mother-in-law unconditionally support [uphold] her son-in-law.)

Ամէն զոքանչ անպայման պիտի իր փեսան գլուխին վրայ դնէ:
Amehn zokanch anbayman beedee eer pesahn klookheen verah teneh.

187 The water went and found the road.
(Returning to your roots. Truth will prevail.)

Ջուրը գնաց եւ ճամբան գտաւ:
Chooruh kenats jahmpahn kdahv.

188 You should have left it the way your father built it.
(You should leave well enough alone.)

Հօրդ շինածովը ձգէիր:
Horuht sheenadzovuh tsekeyeer.

189 If you have fingernails, scratch your head.
(Do for yourself.)

Եթէ եղունգ ունիս՝ գլուխդ քերէ:
Yeteh yeghoonk ooneess, keloukhet kereh.

190 Everything is possible.

Ամէն ինչ հնարաւոր է:
Amen eench henaravohr eh.

191 Whatever you do now, that is what will remain.
(Good deeds don't die.)

Ինչ որ ընես, ատի կը մնայ:
Eench vohr enehss, ahdee guh menah.

192 Don't cry, everything is for us.
(Life has its ups and downs.)

Մի՛ լար, ամէն բան մեզի համար է:
Mee lahr, amen pahn mezee hamar eh.

193 Whatever your stomach wants, eat; otherwise it becomes a negative to your body.

Ինչ որ ՛միտէ՛դ կը քաշէ, կե՛ր, թէ ոչ հակառակ կ՛ըլլայ մարմինիդ:
Eench vohr meedeht guh kahsheh, guehr, teh voch hagarag guhlla marmeeneet.

194 When you are hungry, you will even eat stones.

Երբ սոված լինէք, քարն էլ կ՛ուտէք:
Yerp sovads leenehk, kahrn el goodehk.

195 Don't carry the ladder horizontally. (Don't complicate things.)

Սանդուխը լայնքին մի՛ շալկեր:
Santookhuh laynkeen mee shahlguehr.

Սրտիս սիւնը, հոգիիս բոյնը:

2

Body and Sensory

"The pillar of my heart, the nest of my soul."

Body and Sensory

1 In every person's heart lies hidden a hero.

Ամէն սիրտի մէջ հերոս մը կայ պահուած։
Amen seerdee mech heros muh gah bahvadz.

2 When two mouths become one, they kaka on the one mouth.
(There is strength in numbers.)

Երբ երկու բերան մէկ կ'ըլլան, մէկ բերանին քաք կու տան։
Yerp yergoo peran meg guhllan, meg peraneen kak goodan.

3 They dig the ditch in front of your eye.
(Forethought of malice.)

Փոսը կը փորեն աչքիդ տակ։
Posuh guh poren acheet dahg.

4 They laugh at my face, then they put soap under my feet.
(They act as friends and plan my failure.)

Երեսիս կը խնդան, ոտքիս տակ սապուն (օճառ) կը դնեն։
Yeresees guh khuhntan, vodkees dahg saboon (ojar) guh tuhnen.

5 Soap was put under his foot.
(Evil intent.)

Ոտքին տակ սապուն դրին։
Vodkeen dahg saboon tuhreen.

6 A rock is placed in front of your knee.
(Stumbling block, impediment.)

Ծունկիդ առաջ քար կը ձգէ։
Dzoongeet arach kar guh tsuhkeh.

7 My finger is long; it pierced his eye.
(Curse.)

Մատս երկար է, աչքը մտաւ։
Maduhs yergar eh; achkuh muhdav.

8 He is so cheap that he won't even piss on his injured finger.

Այնքան կծծի է որ վիրաւոր մատին վրայ չի միզեր։
Aynkan guhdzdzee eh vor veeravor madeen vrah chee meezer.

9 Only a handful of soil can satiate the eye of man.
(It's enough, but man wants more.)

Մարդոց աչքը միայն ափ մը հողով կը կշտանայ։
Martots achkuh meeayn ap muh hoghov guh guhshdanah.

10 I have brains, but I don't possess the key to my brains.
(I lack education.)

Խելք ունիմ, բայց խելքիս բանալին չունիմ։
Khelk ooneem, paytz kehlkees panaleen chooneem.

Body and Sensory

11	Fire fell on the heart. (Heartbreak and sudden disaster.)	Կրակ մը ինկաւ սիրտին վրայ։ *Guhrag muh eengav seerdeen vrah.*
12	What you see (know), act like you didn't see (know).	Տեսածդ չտեսածի տեղ դի՛ր։ *Desadzuht chuhdesadzee degh teer.*
13	May my eye go blind. (I am telling you the truth.)	Աչքս քոռնայ։ *Achkuhs kornah.*
14	My eye plays. (Impending danger.)	Աչքս կը խաղայ։ *Achkuhs guh khaghah.*
15	My eye stayed behind. (Lamenting for what might happen.)	Աչքս ետեւը մնաց։ *Achkuhs yedevuh muhnats.*
16	Believe only what your eyes see, only what your ears hear.	Աչքովդ տեսածիդ ու ականջովդ լսածիդ միայն հաւատա՛։ *Achkovuht desadzeet oo aganchovuht luhsadzeet meeayn havadah.*
17	God forbid the loss of your taste buds. (Wishing you well.)	Աստուած բերնիդ համը չկորսնցնէ։ *Asdvadz perneet hamuh chuhgorsuhntsuhneh.*
18	The bread remained in storage and not in the stomach. (The bread was hoarded and never used. Frugality.)	Հացը հորը մնացեր է, փորը չէ մնացած։ *Hatsuh horuh muhnatser eh, poruh cheh muhnatsadz.*
19	May your nipples have holes. (Expression of surprise and well wishes.)	Ծիծերդ ծակծկուին։ *Dzeedzeruht dzagdzuhgveen.*
20	Until your heart feels the pain, your eyes will not tear.	Մինչեւ սիրտդ չի ցաւի, աչքերդ չեն արցունքոտիր։ *Meenchev seerduht chee tsavee, achkeruht chen artsoonkodeer.*
21	The stranger's eye will not bring you light. (Strangers are not concerned.)	Օտարին աչքը քեզի լոյս չի տար։ *Odureen achkuh kezee looys chee dahr.*
22	Even if your jaw were to fall into the water, it wouldn't stop. (You talk too much.)	Ջէնկէդ ջուրն ալ իյնայ, չի կայնիր։ *Chenget choorn al eeynah, chee gayneer.*

23 Two hard heads can make a hole in the wall.
(Stubbornness and unshaken will.)

Երկու տիք գլուխ պատը կը ծակեն:
Yergoo deek kuhlookh baduh guh dzagen.

24 Let what I say be an earring on your ear; don't forget it.

Ասի ականջիդ օղ ըլլայ, մի՛ մոռնար:
Asee agancheet ogh uhllah; mee mornar.

25 Wishes won't come true, accusations will.

Փափաքդ գլուխդ չի գար, բայց մեղադրանքդ կու գայ:
Papakuht kuhlookhuht chee kar, paytz meghatrankuht goo kah.

26 A large head has no brains; large eyes have no light; thick legs have no strength.
(It's not what it seems.)

Մեծ գլուխը կուտ չի կայ, խոշոր աչքին լոյս չի կայ, հաստ ոտքերուն ալ ուժ չի կայ:
Medz kuhlookhuh good chee gah; khoshor achkeen looys chee gah; hasd vodkeroon al oozh chee gah.

27 Was dust blown in his eye?
(Isn't the obvious evident?)

Աչքը թոզ փչեց:
Achkuh toz puhchets?

28 What the eye sees the heart doesn't forget.

Աչքը ինչ որ տեսնէ, սիրտը չի մոռնար:
Achkuh eench vor desneh, seerduh chee mornar.

29 If the blind leads the blind, they will both fall in the pit.

Կոյրը կոյրին եթէ առաջնորդէ, երկուքն ալ կ'իյնան փոսը:
Gooyruh gooyreen yeteh arachnorteh, yergookn al geeynan posuh.

30 If your eye didn't see it, didn't your nose smell it?
(How come you didn't know?)

Աչքդ չտեսաւ, քի՞թդ ալ հոտ չառաւ:
Achkuht chuhdesav, keetuht al hod charav?

31 In the kingdom of the blind, the one-eyed man is king.

Կոյրերու թագաւորութեան մէջ միականին թագաւոր է:
Gooyreroo takavorootyan mech, meeyaganeen takavor eh.

Body and Sensory

32 Instead of opening your mouth, open your eyes.

Բերանդ բանալու տեղ, աչքդ բաց:
Peranuht panaloo degh, achkuht pats.

33 No matter how strong the eye, it cannot rise above the brow.

Աչքդ որքան ալ զօրաւոր ըլլայ, յօնքէն վեր չ'ելլեր:
Achkuh vorkan al zoravor uhllah, honken ver cheller.

34 Better not to have a head than to have a blackened forehead.
(Better not to lose your honor.)

Լաւ է գլուխ չունենալ, քան թէ սեւցած ճակատ մը ունենալ:
Lav eh kuhlookh choonenal, kan teh sevtsadz jagad oonenal.

35 Better to lose your eye than your name (reputation).

Աւելի լաւ է աչքդ կորսնցնես, քան թէ անունդ:
Avelee lav eh achkuht gorsuhntsuhnes, kan teh anoonuht.

36 Better the light go out of a man's eye than his name.

Լաւ է լոյսը մարդուն աչքէն ելլէ, քան թէ անունը:
Lav eh looysuh martoon achken yelleh, kan teh anoonuh.

37 Your lips won't wear out by kissing someone's hand.
(Showing respect won't hurt you.)

Ձեռք համբուրելով շրթունքդ չի մաշիր:
Tserk hampoorelov shuhrtoonkuht chee masheer.

38 What the right hand gives the left doesn't know.

Աջ ձեռքիդ տուածը ձախը չ'իմանար:
Ach tserkeet duhvadzuh tsakhuh cheemanar.

39 From every one finger drip ten talents.
(Endowed with many talents.)

Ամէն մէկ մատէն տասը հիւներ կը թափի:
Amen meg maden dasuh hyooner guh tahpee.

40 Ten fingers, ten talents.
(Talented.)

Տասը մատ, տասը հիւներ:
Dasuh mad, dasuh hyooner.

41 One hand cannot clap.

Մէկ ձեռքը ծափ չի տար:
Meg tserkuh dzap chee dahr.

42 If one hand washes the other hand, then two hands can wash your face.
(There is strength in cooperation.)

Ձեռքդ ձեռքիդ եթէ լուայ, երկու ձեռքդ ալ երեսդ կը լուայ:
Tserkuht tserkeet yeteh luhvah, yergoo tserkuht al yeresuht guh luhvah

43 What does one hand have? Two hands can make noise.

Մէկ ձեռքը ի՞նչ ունի, երկու ձեռքը ձայն ունի:
Meg tserkuh eench oonee? Yergoo tserkuh tsayn oonee.

44 May God not allow your right hand to depend on your left hand.
(May God keep you independent.)

Աստուած աջ ձեռքդ ձախ ձեռքիդ չձգէ:
Asdvadz ach tserkuht tsakh tserkeet chuhtsuhkeh.

45 Black heart, white tooth.
(Don't be misled by evil.)

Սեւ սիրտ - ճերմակ ակռայ:
Sev seerd, jermag agrah.

46 The heart is a glass palace; when it shatters, it can't be fixed.

Սիրտը ապակիէ պալատ է, երբ կոտրի, չի շինուիր:
Seerduh abageeyeh balad eh; yerp godree, chee sheenveer.

47 Which one of your fingers must you cut, not to experience pain?

Ո՞ր մէկ մատդ կտրես, որ չցաւի:
Vor meg maduht guhdres, vor chuhtsavee?

48 The tear is a language that only one who cries can understand.

Արցունքը լեզու մըն է, ան որ կու լայ միայն կը հասկնայ:
Artsoonkuh lezoo muhn eh; an vor goolah meeayn guh hasguhnah.

49 The liar has a long tongue.
(The liar speaks many falsehoods.)

Սուտ խօսողին լեզուն երկար կ'ըլլայ:
Sood khosogheen lezoon yergar guhllah.

50 Far from the eye, far from the heart.
(Out of sight, out of mind.)

Աչքէ հեռու, սիրտէ հեռու:
Achkeh heroo, seerdeh heroo.

51 My heart is not a tablecloth to spread on everything.
(I have been drained and used.)

Իմ սիրտս սեղանի լաթ չէ, որ ամէն բանի վրայ փռես:
Eem seerduhs seghanee lat cheh, vor amen panee vrah puhres.

Body and Sensory

52 She gossips between two eyes and two eyebrows.
(She doesn't miss a chance to gossip.)

Երկու աչքին ու յօնքին արան կը բամբասէ:
Yergoo achkeen oo honkeen aran guh pampaseh.

53 The tongue oftentimes breaks the head.
(The tongue is a lethal weapon.)

Լեզուն շատ անգամ կը կոտրէ գլուխը:
Lezoon shad ankam guh godreh kulookhuh.

54 There are two things you can't stare at with your eyes: the sun and death.

Երկու բան կայ որ կարելի չէ աչքերը սեւեռած դիտել, արեւը եւ մահը:
Yergoo pan gah vor garelee cheh achkeruh severadz teedel- arevuh yev mahuh.

55 A sound mind in a sound body.

Առողջ միտք առողջ մարմինին:
Arokhch meedk, arokhch marmeeneen.

56 When you have a bad tooth, pull it out and be free. When you have a bad neighbor, pull away and be free.

Գէշ ակռայ եթէ ունիս, քաշէ՛, հանէ՛, ազատի՛ր: Գէշ դրացի եթէ ունիս, քաշուէ՛, գնա՛, ազատի՛ր:
Kesh agrah yeteh oonees, kasheh haneh, azadeer. Kesh tuhratsee yeteh oonees, kashveh kuhnah, azadeer.

57 The thief's heart trembles.

Գող, սիրտը դող:
Kogh, seerduh togh.

58 You have a place on top of my head.
(You are special to me.)

Գլխուս վրայ տեղ ունիս:
Kulkhoos vrah degh oonees.

59 My forehead is open.
(I have nothing to hide.)

Ճակատս բաց է:
Jagaduhs pats eh.

60 Hair long, brain short.

Մազը երկար, խելքը կարճ:
Mazuh yergar, khelkuh garj.

61 Clench your teeth.
(Persevere.)

Ակռադ սեղմէ:
Agrat seghmeh.

62 What the teeth cut he eats.
(Glutton.)

Ակռային կտրածը կ'ուտէ:
Agrayeen guhdradzuh goodeh.

63 May the sin be on your neck. (Don't blame me. You are responsible.)	Մեղքդ վիզդ ըլլայ։ *Mekhkuht veezuht uhllah.*
64 Wraps it around his finger. (He is a manipulator.)	Մատին վրայ կը փաթթէ։ *Madeen vrah guh patteh.*
65 He plays one on the finger. (Manipulates.)	Մատին վրայ կը խաղցնէ։ *Madeen vrah guh khaghtsuhneh.*
66 Searches my mouth. (Wants information.)	Բերանս կը փնտռէ։ *Peranuhs guh puhndreh.*
67 Eye has a hole. (Greed, never sated.)	Աչքը ծակ է։ *Achkuh dzag eh.*
68 Hang a blue bead to avoid the evil eye. (A superstitious belief that the blue bead protects from evil.)	Կապոյտ ուլունք կախէ, որ աչքի չի գայ։ *Gabooyd ooloonk gakheh, vor achkee chee kah.*
69 His eye darkened. (Evil eye.)	Աչքը սեւցաւ։ *Achkuh sevtsav.*
70 My blood turned to water. (I was frightened.)	Արիւնս ջուր կտրեցաւ։ *Aryoonuhs choor guhdretzav.*
71 He is a dry head. (He is stubborn.)	Չոր գլուխ է։ *Chor kuhlookh eh.*
72 I didn't smell my finger. (I didn't take the hint.)	Մատս չհոտուըտացի։ *Maduhs chuhodvuhdatsee.*
73 Came out of the eye. (Fell out of favor.)	Աչքէն ելաւ։ *Achken yelav.*
74 Don't hang an ear. (Don't heed.)	Ականջ մի՛ կախեր։ *Aganch mee gakher.*
75 Don't give face. (Don't spoil.)	Երես մի՛ տար։ Yeres mee dahr.
76 One who touches the honey licks his finger.	Մեղրին դպչողը մատը կը լզէ։ *Meghreen tuhboghuh maduh guh luhzeh.*

77 Entered the eye.
(Gained favor.)

Աչքը մտաւ:
Achkuh medav.

78 The money of the rich is the tongue for the poor.
(The poor is the beggar.)

Հարուստին դրամը աղքատին լեզուն է:
Haroosdeen tuhramuh aghkadeen lezoon eh.

79 Light candles on ten fingers; it won't help.
(They don't get it.)

Տասը մատը մոմ վառէ, նորէն օգուտ չունի:
Dasuh maduh mom vareh, noren okood choonee.

80 I blackened my face, asked for what was owed to me.
(I embarrassed myself when I asked for my money.)

Երեսս սեւցուցի, առնելիքս ուզեցի:
Yeresuhs sevtsootsee, arneleekuhs oozetsee

81 Man's face is the mirror of his heart.

Դէմքը մարդուն սիրտին հայելին է:
Temkuh martoon seerdeen hayeleen eh.

82 Close one eye and one ear.
(Be forgiving.)

Մէկ աչքդ, մէկ ականջդ գոցէ:
Meg achkuht, meg aganchuht kotseh.

83 He who does not hear (understand) with his ear will hear (understand) with his back (stick).

Ան որ չի լսեր ականջով, կը լսէ կռնակով:
Ahn vor chee luhssehr aganchov, guh luhsseh guhrnagov.

84 Whatever you learn is a gold bracelet on your arm.

Ինչ որ սորվիս, ձեռքիդ վրայ, ոսկի ապարանջան է:
Eench vor sorvees, tserkeet vrah vosgee abaranchan eh.

85 When you have too much butter, you brush it on your buttocks.
(When you have too much, you become extravagant.)

Եթէ շատ կարագ ունենաս, ոռիդ (յետոյքիդ) կը քսես:
Yeteh shad garak oonenas, voreet guh kuhses.

86 Stretch your feet to the length of your quilt, roll your quilt to the length of your feet.
(Live according to your means.)

Ոտքդ վերմակիդ համեմատ երկարէ, վերմակդ ոտքիդ չափ ոլորէ:
Vodkuht vermageet hamemad yergareh, vermaguht vodkeet chap voloreh.

87 Don't stick your foot out of the quilt
(Don't live beyond your means.)

Ոտքդ վերմակէդ դուրս մի՛ հաներ:
Vodkuht vermageht toors mee haner.

88 One who lacks sensitivity digs the ditch for another, and the dirt falls on his own head.
(He is insensitive to others and suffers the consequences.)

Զգացում չունեցողը ուրիշին հողը կը փորէ, ու հողը իր գլխուն կը թափի:
Uhzkatsoom choonetsoghuh ooreesheen hoghuh guh poreh, oo hoghuh eer kuhlkhhoon guh tapee.

89 Don't throw a stone up; it will fall on your head on its way down.

Դուն մի՛ նետեր վեր քար, դարձին կ'իյնայ գլխուդ վար:
Toon mee neder ver kar, tartseen geeynah kuhlkhoot var.

90 One who enters the dance must shake his buttocks.
(Commitment involves participation. Roll with the punches.)

Պարի մտնողը ոռը պիտի շարժէ:
Baree muhdnoghuh voruh beedee sharzheh.

91 Judgment came from your own mouth.

Ի բերնէ քումմէ դատուեցար:
Ee perneh koommeh tadvetsar.

92 Doesn't see the beam in his eye, sees the sliver in the eyes of others.

Իր աչքին գերանը չի տեսներ, ուրիշին աչքին շիւղը կը տեսնէ:
Eer achkeen keranuh chee dessner, ooreesheen achkeen shyooghuh guh desneh.

93 The meat for you, the bone for me.
(You have full authority; I will sacrifice for you.)

Միսը՝ քեզի, ոսկորը՝ ինծի:
Meesuh kezee, vosgoruh eendzee.

94 Instead of a finger measure of a father, have a thimble full of a mother.
(A mother can do more with less.)

Փոխանակ մատի չափ հայր ունենալու, մատնոցի չափ մայր ունեցիր:
Pokhanag madee chap hayr oonenaloo, madnotsee chap mayr oonetseer.

95 If you like me, go bring your mother's heart.
(Twisted test of love.)

Ինծի կը սիրե՞ս, գնա՛ մայրիկիդ սիրտը բեր:
Eendzee guh seeres, kuhnah mayreegeet seerduh per.

96 The son who takes his mother's heart will take two hearts from his wife.
(He will aggravate his wife's heart twice as much.)

Այն զաւակը որ մօրը սիրտը կ'առնէ, կնոջ երկուքը կ'առնէ:
Ayn zavaguh vor moruh seerduh garneh, gunoch yergookuh garneh.

97 In the parade two buttocks touched and they became related.
(Armenians become kindred souls upon meeting.)

Երկու յետոյքները տողանցքի ժամանակ իրարու դպան ու ազգական դարձան:
Yergoo hedooykner doghantskee zhamanag eeraroo tuhban oo askagan tartsan.

98 If the child is not spanked, the knee will be slapped.
(One who does not spank the child will slap his own knee in regret.)

Ան որ չօճուխին չի ծեծեր, ծունկին կը զարնէ:
Ahn vor chojookheen chee dzedzer, dzoongeen guh zarneh.

99 A woman who loses her husband is like a woman whose backbone is broken.

Ամուսինը կորսնցնող կին մը ողնայարը կոտրած կնոջ կը նմանի:
Amooseenuh gorsuntsuhnogh geen muh voghanharuh godradz guhnoch guh nuhmanee.

100 The do-gooder's beard is kakaed.
(Goodness is unappreciated.)

Շատ ընողին մօրուքը կը քաքնեն:
Shad uhnogheen morookuh guh kaknen.

101 May God not allow the one under your foot (an underling) to be over your head.

Աստուած չձգէ որ ոտքիդ տակինը գլուխիդ վրայ ըլլայ:
Asdvadz chuhtsuhkeh vor vodkeet dageenuh kuhlookheet vrah uhllah.

102 Let me die without begging for a drop of water; may God not deprive me of my hands and feet.

Կաթիլ մը ջուր չուզած մեռնիմ, Աստուած ձեռքէ, ոտքէ չձգէ:
Gateel muh choor choozadz merneem, Asdvadz tserkeh, vodkeh chuhtsuhkeh.

103 I put my live head under the Gospel.
(Responsibility of commitment.)

Ողջ գլուխս Աւետարանի տակ դրի:
Voghch kuhlookhuhs Avedaranee dag tuhree.

104 When God gives, He gives with two hands.	Երբ Աստուած կու տայ, երկու ձեռքով կու տայ: *Yerp Asdvadz goo dah, yergoo tserkov goo dah.*
105 God has a finger to stick in your eye. (Curse.)	Աստուած մատ ունի որ աչքդ խոթէ: *Asdvadz mahd oonee, vor achkuht khoteh!*
106 I haven't eaten onion, so my stomach can't hurt. (There is no fear with prevention.)	Սոխ չեմ կերած որ փորս ցաւի: *Sokh chem geradz vor poruhs tsavee.*
107 A sweet tongue will draw the snake from the hole.	Անուշ լեզուն օձը ծակէն կը հանէ: *Anoosh lezoon otsuh dzagen guh haneh.*
108 The horse was whipped, did his teeth fall out? (Exaggeration.)	Ձին պարկին ակռա՞ն ինկաւ: *Tseen zargeen, agran eengav?*
109 The fish dies through its mouth. (Gossip hurts.)	Ձուկը բերնէն կը մեռնի: *Tsooguh pernen guh mernee.*
110 The fish rotted from the head. (Corruption starts from the top.)	Ձուկը գլուխէն հոտեր է: *Tsooguh kuhlookhen hoder eh.*
111 It was asked of the fish, "What news do you have from the sea?" The fish said, "I have much to say, but my mouth is full of water." (Ask the person who knows.)	Ձուկին հարցուցին, «Ծովէն ի՞նչ լուր», ըսաւ, «Շատ բան ունիմ ըսելիք, բայց բերանս ջուրով լեցուն է»: *Tsoogeen hartsootseen, "Dzovehn eench loor?" Uhsav, "Shahd pahn ooneem uhsseleek, payts peranuhs choorov letsoon eh."*
112 Raise the black crow, so it will gouge your eye out. (Do good, and get evil in return.)	Սեւ ղուշը մեծցու՛ր որ աչքդ փորէ: *Sev ghooshuh medztsoor vor achkuht poreh.*
113 Ant or bird without a nose (to direct) can't fly. (Knowledge is necessary.)	Մրջիւն, թռչուն քիթերսուզ չեն թռիր: *Muhrchyoon, tuhrchoon keetersooz chen tuhreer.*
114 You can't catch a bird with one hand.	Մէկ ձեռքով թռչուն չի բռնուիր: *Meg tserkov tuhrchoon chee puhrnuhveer.*

115 Every sheep is hung by its feet.
(Right way to do things.)

Ամէն ոչխար իր ոտքէն կը կախեն:
Amen vochkhar eer vodken guh gakhen.

116 It was asked of the camel, "Why is your neck crooked?" The camel replied, "What part of me is straight, that my neck should be, too?"

Ուղտին ըսեր են, «Ինչո՞ւ վիզդ ծուռ է», ուղտը ըսեր է, «Իմ ո՞րտեղս շիտակ է, որ վիզս ալ շիտակ ըլլայ»:
Ooghdeen uhser en, "Eenchoo veezuht dzoor eh? Ooghduh uhser eh, "Eem vordeghuhs sheedag eh, vor veezuhs al sheedag uhllah?"

117 The cat cannot reach the liver, so he says it's spoiled.
(Sour grapes.)

Կատուն ճիկէրին չի հասնիր, հոտած է կ'ըսէ:
Gadoon jeegereen chee hasneer, hodadz eh guhseh.

118 In every heart there is a lion.

Ամէն սրտի մէջ առիւծ մը կայ:
Amen suhrdee mech aryoodz muh gah.

119 The pillar of my heart, the nest of my soul.
(Endearment.)

Սրտիս սիւնը, հոգիիս բոյնը:
Suhrdees syoonuh, hokeeyees pooynuh.

120 The orphan poured water on his head, heaven and earth darkened.
(Unfortunate.)

Որբը գլուխը ջուր դրեր է, երկինք եւ գետին մթներ են:
Vorpuh kuhlookhuh choor tuhrer eh, yergeenk yev kedeen muhtner en.

121 Citizenship is enjoyable, if you have money in your hands.

Քաղաքացիութիւնը համ ունի, երբ որ ձեռքդ դրամ ունիս:
Kaghakatseeyootyoonuh ham oonee, yerp vor tserkuht tuhram oonees.

122 With joyfulness the hair grows long, with sadness the fingernails.
(Joy brings growth, sadness brings neglect.)

Ուրախութենէն մազը կ'երկարի, տխրութենէն՝ եղունգը:
Oorakhootenen mazuh gergaree, duhkhrootenen yeghoonkuh.

123 If you hold his nose, will his spirit come out?
(Exaggerated outcome.)

Քիթը բռնես, հոգի՞ն կ'ելլէ:
Keetuh puhrnes, hokeen gelleh?

124 From every head comes a sound.
(Different opinions.)

Ամէն գլուխէն ձայն մը կ՚ելլէ:
Amen kuhlookhehn tsayn muh gelleh.

125 When the pot overboils, the heat overflows on its own head.
(Unwise decisions have consequences.)

Պտուկը, եթէ եփի, կրակը իր գլխուն վրայ կը լեցուի:
Buhdooguh, yeteh yepee, guhraguh eer kuhlkhoon vrah guh letsvee.

126 The tongue has no bone.
(The tongue is loose. Gossip.)

Լեզուն ոսկոր չունի:
Lezoon vosgor choonee.

127 Hair has grown on my tongue.
(I nagged but to no avail.)

Լեզուիս վրայ մազ բուսաւ:
Lezvees vrah maz poosav.

128 Can't wash blood away with blood.
(No-win situation.)

Արիւնը արիւնով չի լուացուիր:
Aryoonuh aryoonov chee luhvatsveer.

129 Wash the feet, drink the water.
(Gratitude; thankfulness with humility.)

Ոտքը լուա՛, ջո՛ւրը խմէ:
Vodkuh luhvah, chooruh khuhmeh.

130 If your ten fingers are lit like candles, they still will not understand.

Տասը մատդ մոմ ըլլայ եւ ամբողջը վառի, նորէն չեն տեսներ:
Dasuh maduht mom uhllah yev ampokhch varee, noren chen dessnehr.

131 Spit in his face, he thinks the rain is coming.
(Insensitive; no shame.)

Երեսը թքնես, կը խորհի անձրեւ կու գայ:
Yeresuh tuhknes, guh khorhee antsrev goo kah.

132 If you spit up, it's your ceiling; if you spit down, it's your beard.
(No-win situation.)

Վեր թքնես՝ տանիքդ է, վար թքնես՝ մօրուքդ է:
Ver tuhknes, daneekuht eh; var tuhknes, morookuht eh.

133 Where there is bread, there is no mouth (hunger); where there is mouth (hunger), there is no bread.
(Needs not fulfilled.)

Ուր հաց կայ, բերան չի կայ, ուր բերան կայ, հաց չի կայ:
Oor hats gah, peran chee gah; oor peran gah, hats chee gah.

134 Looks for hairs in the eggs.
(Fussy, persnickety.)

Հաւկիթին մէջ մազ կը փնտռէ:
Havgeeteen mech maz guh puhndreh.

135 Burned his mouth on hot milk, so he blows on the yogurt.
(Hesitant, taking precautionary measures.)

Կաթէն բերանը այրեցաւ, մածունին վրայ կը փչէ:
Gahten peranuh ayretsav, madzooneen vrah guh puhcheh.

136 A man who has burned his tongue on hot milk will find himself blowing on yogurt.
(Fearful because of past experience.)

Այն մարդը որ լեզուն կ'այրէ տաք կաթէն, կը փչէ մածունին վրայ:
Ayn martuh vor lezoon gayreh dahk gahten, guh puhcheh madzooneen vra.

137 The empty wheat stalk raises its head.
(No substance.)

Պարապ ցորենի հասկը գլուխը կը բարձրացնէ:
Barab tsorenee hasguh kuhlookhuh guh partsratsuhneh.

138 He who falls in the sea will reach for the foam.
(Desperation.)

Ծովն ինկողը ձեռքը փրփուրին կը նետէ:
Dzovn eengoghuh tserkuh puhrpooreen guh nedeh.

139 Wish well for your neighbor, so goodness will come to your head.

Բարի ուզէ դրացիիդ, որ բարի գայ գլխուդ:
Paree oozeh tuhratseeyeet, vor paree kah kuhlkhoot.

140 Your friend looks at your head, your enemy at your feet.
(Your friend can look you in the eye, your enemy cannot.)

Բարեկամդ գլխուդ կը նայի, թշնամիդ՝ ոտքիդ:
Paregamuht kuhlkhoot guh nayee, tuhshnameet vodkeet.

141 Our real grave is not in the ground but in the hearts of people.

Մեր իրական գերեզմանը հողին մէջ չէ, այլ մարդոց սրտին մէջ:
Mer eeragan kerezmanuh hogheen mech cheh, ayl martots seerdeen mech.

142 Hope remained in the stomach.
(Unfulfilled.)

Փափաքը փորը մնաց:
Papakuh poruh muhnats.

143 Fed with a spoon, removed the eye with the handle.
(Goodness obliterated by evildoing.)

Դգալով կերցուց, կոթով աչքը հանեց:
Tuhkalov gertsoots, gotov achkuh hanets.

144 When a poor man extends his hand, it's not for greeting.

Երբ աղքատ մը ձեռքը կ'երկնցնէ, բարեւելու համար չէ:
Yerp aghkad muh tserkuh gerguhntsuhneh, pareveloo hamar cheh.

145 It's hanging over my head like a Damoclean sword.
(Burdened; dangerous or precarious situation.)

Դամոկլեսեան սուրի պէս գլխուս վրայ կախուած է:
Tamoglesian sooreen bes kuhlkhoos vrah gakhvadz eh.

146 Laughter is abundant in the mouth of fools.

Խնդուքը առատ է ապուշներուն բերնին մէջ:
Khuntookuh arad eh abooshneroon perneen mech.

147 The walls have ears.
(A warning that someone could be eavesdropping.)

Պատերը ականջ ունին:
Bahderuh aganch ooneen.

148 He doesn't bring to a head.
(Does not bring to fruition.)

Գլուխ չի բերեր:
Kloukh chee perer.

149 My heart burns.
(Emotional pain.)

Սիրտս կը վառի:
Seerduhs guh varee.

150 He plants potatoes in his ear.
(He doesn't listen.)

Ականջը փաթաթէս կը ցանէ:
Aganchuh patates guh tsaneh.

151 He doesn't have face.
(No shame.)

Երես չունի:
Yeres choonee.

152 Whatever your stomach wants, eat; otherwise it becomes a negative to your body.

Ինչ որ 'միտէ'դ կը քաշէ, կե'ր, թէ ոչ հակառակ կ'ըլլայ մարմինիդ:
Eench vohr meedeht guh kahsheh, guehr, teh voch hagarag guhlla marmeeneet.

153 My mind is not at rest.
(I don't get it, not logical.)

Խելքիս չի պառկիր:
Khelkees chee bargueer.

154 He did it with his hand.
(It's his own fault.)

Իրեն ձեռքով ըրաւ:
Eeren tserkov erav.

155 Is your hand for rent?
(Lazy.)

Ձեռքդ վարձո՞ւ է:
Tserkuht vartsoo ye?

156 (He) exhausts the heart.
(Wears out or stresses out others.)

Սիրտ կը հատցնէ:
Seerd guh hadtseneh.

157 Scratch your buttocks.
(To ward off evil eye.)

Ոռդ քերէ:
Vohruht kereh.

158 Upstairs is empty.
(No brains.)

Վերը պարապ է:
Veruh barahb eh.

159 His eye was left in it.
(Unfulfilled.)

Աչքը մէջը մնաց:
Achkuh mechuh mnats.

160 His nose is crooked.
(Angry.)

Քիթը ծուռ է:
Keetuh dzoor eh.

161 The man is the head, the wife is the neck.
(Woman controls.)

Մարդը գլուխն է, կինը վիզն է:
Martuh klookhn eh, gueenuh veezn eh.

162 Black heart.
(Evil heart; ill wisher.)

Սեւ սիրտ:
Sev seerd.

163 (May) your sin remain on your neck.
(It's your fault, your responsibility.)

Մեղքդ վիզդ մնայ:
Meghkuh veezuht mna.

164 If you have fingernails, scratch your head.
(Do for yourself.)

Եթէ եղունգ ունիս՝ գլուխդ քերէ:
Yeteh yeghoonk ooneess keloukhet kereh.

165 Two hands do the clapping.
(Cooperation.)

Երկու ձեռք կը ծափահարեն:
Yergoo tserk guh dzapaharen.

166 When they are giving money, they are shaking.
(They are stingy.)

Փարայ պիտի տան՝ կը դողան:
Para beedee dahn, guh toghahn.

167 His face is torn.
(Shameless.)

Երեսը պատռած է:
Yeressuh bahdradz eh.

168 They have no taste in their mouth.
(Clueless, and don't know what's good for them.)

Բերանին համը չեն գիտեր:
Peraneen hamuh chen keeder.

169 Let them explode, let their nose be mired (in mud).
(Let them be humiliated; let them suffer.)

Թող ճաթին, քիթերնին թող քսուի:
Togh jahteen, keeterneen togh kessvee.

170 His mind and brain are mixed with kaka.
(He is crazy, confused.)

Միտքը խելքը քաքին հետ խառնուած է:
Mitkuh, khelkuh kahkeen hed kharnevadz eh.

171 My mind flew.
(I forgot.)

Խելքս թռաւ:
Khelkuhs trahv.

172 From mouth to mouth a mote becomes a log.
(Gossip, exaggeration.)

Բերնէ բերան՝ կ'ըլլայ գերան:
Perneh perahn, guehlla kerahn.

173 He speaks under his nose.
(Insincere.)

Քիթին տակէն կը խօսի:
Keeteen dahguen guh khossee.

174 He took my pity, wrapped it around my neck.
(I took on his problems.)

Խիղճս առաւ, վիզս փաթթեց:
Kheeghjuhs arav, veezuhs pattets.

175 (She) is with liver.
(In Armenia, liver is equivalent to the heart. It means she cares for people.)

Ճիկէրով է:
Jiguerohv eh.

176 (He) drained the blood.
(He drained the emotions.)

Արիւն քամեց:
Aryun kahmets.

177 (He) has fallen from his nose.
(He is a clone of his father.)

Քիթէն ինկեր է:
Keetehn eenguer eh.

178 My brain is not in my head.
(I can't think.)

Խելքս գլուխս չէ:
Khelkuhs klookhuhs cheh.

179 Pumpkin head.
(Not smart.)

Դդում գլուխ:
Tetoom kelookh.

180 He who gossips in front of you will also gossip behind you.

Առջեւդ խօսողը՝ ետեւդ ալ կը խօսի:
Archevuht khossoghuh, yedevuht ahl guh khossee.

181 When afflicted with stress (fright, terror), it affects the weakest part of the body.

Սոսկումը ունենաս, նապիկ տեղը կը բռնէ:
Sosgoomuh oonenahs, nahzeeg deghuh guh perneh.

182 Puts his hand in his pocket, it goes to his ass.
(Empty pocket; broke.)

Ձեռքը գրպանը կը դնէ, ոռը կ'երթայ:
Tzerkuh kerbanuh guh teneh, voruh guerta.

183 The luck of the lazy man comes and sits on his knee.
(Luck falls on the lazy.)

Ծոյլ մարդուն բաղդը կու գայ ծունկին կը նստի:
Dzooyl mahrtoon paghtuh gooka dzoongueen vrah guh nesdee.

184 Pear head.
(Stupid.)

Տանձի գլուխ:
Dantsee kelookh.

185 They judge man from the eye of the needle.
(Extreme fault-finding.)

Ասեղին ծակէն մարդ կը դիտեն:
Asegheen dzagen mart guh teeden.

186 You don't butt your head with a fool.
(Can't waste time reasoning with a fool.)

Խենթին հետ գլուխ չես դներ:
Khenteen hed kuhlookh ches tuhner.

187 The soul is willing, the body is weak.

Հոգին յօժար է, մարմինը տկար է:
Hokeesn hojar eh, marmeenus dgar eh.

188 Every mother-in-law must put her son-in-law on her head.
(Let every mother-in-law unconditionally support [uphold] her son-in-law.)

Ամէն կոքանչ անպայման պիտի իր փեսան գլուխին վրայ դնէ:
Amehn zokanch anbayman beedee eer pesahn klookheen verah teneh.

189 Stretch your feet to the length of your quilt, roll your quilt to the length of your feet.
(Live according to your means.)

Ոտքդ վերմակիդ համեմատ երկարէ, վերմակդ ոտքիդ չափ ոլորէ:
Vodkuht vermageet hamemad yergareh, vermaguht vodkeet chap voloreh.

Զաւակը ծաղիկ մըն է, վրան կը նայիս կ'ուրախանաս:

3

Family

"Your child is like a flower, to look upon and be joyful."

Family

1	Instead of a finger measure of a father, have a thimble full of a mother. (A mother can do more with less.)	Փոխանակ մատի չափ հայր ունենալու, մատնոցի չափ մայր ունեցիր: *Pokhanag madee chap hayr oonenaloo, madnotsee chap mayr oonetseer.*
2	Instead of my mother crying, let your mother cry.	Իմ մայրս լալու, քու մայրդ թող լայ: *Eem mayruhs laloo, koo mayruht togh lah.*
3	If you like me, go bring your mother's heart. (Twisted test of love.)	Ինծի կը սիրե՞ս, գնա՛ մայրիկիդ սիրտը բե՛ր: *Eendzee guh seeres, kuhnah mayreegeet seerduh per.*
4	The son who takes his mother's heart will take two hearts from his wife. (He will aggravate his wife's heart twice as much.)	Այն պաւակը որ մօրը սիրտը կ'առնէ, կնոջը երկուքը կ'առնէ: *Ayn zavaguh vor moruh seerduh garneh, guhnoch yergookuh garneh.*
5	The father is the flood, the mother is the dam. (The father is the spender, the mother is the conserver.)	Հայրը սել է, մայրը պէնտ է: *Hayruh sel eh, mayruh bend eh.*
6	A mother can take care of ten children, a father can't take care of himself.	Մայր մը տասը պաւակ կրնայ կառավարել, հայր մը ինքզինք չի կրնար կառավարել: *Mayr muh dasuh zavag guhrnah garavarel, hayr muh eenkzeenk chee guhrnar garavarel.*
7	One mother can manage ten children, but one child cannot manage its own mother.	Մայր մը տասը չօճուխ կրնայ կառավարել, բայց մէկ չօճուխ մը մէկ մայր չի կրնար կառավարել: *Mayr muh dasuh chojookh guhrnah garavarel, payts meg chojookh muh meg mayr chee guhrnar garavarel.*
8	A woman who loses her husband is like a woman whose backbone is broken.	Ամուսինը կորսնցնող կին մը ողնայարը կոտրած կնոջ կը նմանի: *Amooseenuh gorsuhntsuhnogh geen muh voghnaharuh godradz guhnoch guh nuhmanee.*

9 The mother hasn't eaten, the mother hasn't eaten, the eggs of twelve children, half she has eaten.
(The mother complains but eats more than her share.)

Մայր մը չէ կերեր, մայր մը չէ կերեր, տասներկու չօճուխին կէսն է կերեր:
Mayr muh che gerer, mayr muh cheh gerer, 12 chojookheen havgeeteen gesn eh gerer.

10 When buying cloth, look at the selvage; when marrying a girl, look at the mother.
(The daughter is what the mother is.)

Պասմա առնես՝ եզերքը նայէ՛, աղջիկ առնես՝ մօրը նայէ:
Basmah arnes, yezerkuh nayeh; aghcheeg arnes, moruh nayeh.

11 The son sold his mother's homespun.
(Son undersells his mother's worthy labor; opportunist.)

Մօրը մանածը ծախած է:
Moruh manadzuh dzakhadz eh.

12 In the parade two buttocks touched and they became related.
(Armenians become kindred souls upon meeting.)

Երկու յետոյքներ տողանցքի ժամանակ իրարու դպան ու ազգական եղան:
Yergoo hedooykner doghantskee zhamanag eeraroo tuhban oo azkagan tartsan.

13 Those who have children don't need enemies.

Զաւակ ունեցողը թշնամիի պէտք չունի:
Zavag oonetsoghuh tuhshnameeyee bedk choonee.

14 The baby who doesn't cry doesn't get milk.

Չի լացող պզտիկը կաթ չ'ունենար:
Chee latsogh buhzdeeguh gat choonenar.

15 Gave birth to the child, didn't give birth to the nature.
(The temperament of the child is not the parent's responsibility.)

Զաւակը բերի, բնութիւնը չի բերի:
Zavaguh peree, puhnootyoonuh chee peree.

16 If the child is not spanked, the knee will be slapped.
(One who doesn't spank the child will slap his own knee in regret.)

Ան որ չօճուխին չի ծեծեր, ծունկին կը զարնէ:
Ahn vor chojookheen chee dzedzer, dzoongeen guh zarneh.

17 Mother makes bread, baby is crying.
(Mother's work is never done; multi-tasking.)

Մաման հաց, ճաղան լաց:
Maman hahts, chaghan lahts.

18 Don't be fooled by a woman's beauty; rather, let her character be beautiful.

Կնոջ մը գեղեցկութեան մի՛ խաբուիր, թող բնութիւնը գեղեցիկ ըլլայ:
Guhnoch muh keghetsgootyan mee khapveer; togh puhnootyoonuh keghetseeg uhllah.

19 Let them be alive and well, but let them stay in their place.
(We wish them well, but let them stay out of our lives.)

Ողջ ըլլան, լաւ ըլլան, տեղերնին մնան:
Voghch uhllan, lav uhllan, degherneen muhnan.

20 A mother's fortune is the daughter's collar.
(The mother is fortunate if the daughter marries well.)

Մօրը բախտը աղջկան օձիք:
Moruh pakhduh, aghchuhgan otseeg.

21 Little ones, little problems; when they get big, big problems.

Պստիկներ պստիկ պէլա, մեծ ըլլան մեծ պէլա:
Buhzdeegner, buhzdeeg belah, medz uhllahn medz belah.

22 (My) daughter, I'll tell you; daughter-in-law, you understand.
(The father speaks through the daughter to the daughter-in-law.)

Աղջիկս քեզի կ'ըսեմ, հարս դուն հասկցիր:
Aghcheeguhs, kezee uhsem, hars toon hasguhtseer.

23 The shade of the son-in-law, the shade of the thorn.
(No benefit from either one.)

Փեսային շուքն է, փուշին շուքն է:
Pesayeen shookn eh, poosheen shookn eh.

24 Before a son, now a neighbor.
(Marriage separates the bond.)

Առաջ տղաս էիր, հիմա դրացիս ես:
Arach duhghas eyeer, himah tuhratsees ehs.

25 A girl can be more worthy than seven boys.

Աղջիկ կայ եօթը տղայ կ'արժէ:
Aghcheeg gah vor yotuh duhghah garzheh.

26 Marriage is an iron yoke.

Ամուսնութիւնը երկաթէ լուծ է:
Amoosnootyoonuh yergateh loodz eh.

27 Every pot finds its lid.
(Perfect match in marriage.)

Ամէն թէնճէրէ իր ղափաղը կը գտնէ:
Amen tenjereh eer ghapaghuh guh kuhdneh.

28 The child is yours until noon; the husband is yours until night. (The child is yours until marriage, but the husband is yours forever.)

Զաւակդ քուկդ է մինչեւ ցերեկ, ամուսինդ քուկդ է մինչեւ գիշեր։
Zavaguht kooguht eh meenchev tsoreg, amooseenuht kooguht eh meenchev keesher.

29 When you send a child for water, spank him first, then send him; after the cup is broken, it's no use.

Երեխան երբ ջուրի ղրկես, նախ ծեծէ, վերջը ղրկէ. գաւաթը կոտրելէն վերջ բան չ'արժեր։
Yerekhan yerp chooree ghuhrges, nakh dzedzeh, verchuh ghuhrgeh; kavatuh godrelen verch pan charzher.

30 Man's luck doesn't change, his pillow changes. (A second marriage will not change your luck.)

Մարդուն բախտը չի փոխուիր, բարձը կը փոխուի։
Martoon pakhduh chee pokhveer, partsuh guh pokhvee.

31 It can't be digested, even with onions and garlic. (Unlikely matrimonial match.)

Սոխ ու սխտորով ալ չի մարսուիր։
Sokh oo suhkhdorov al chee marsuhveer.

32 May you grow old on one pillow. (A wedding toast for a long happy marriage.)

Մէկ բարձի վրայ ծերանաք։
Meg partsee vrah dzeranak.

33 The rolling jar went and found its lid. (Perfect match in marriage.)

Գլորուեցաւ պտուկը, գնաց գտաւ խուփիկը։
Kuhlorvetsav buhdooguh, kuhnats kuhdav khoopeeguh.

34 Leaving your husband doesn't change your luck; only your pillow changes.

Էրիկ ձգելէն բախտդ չի փոխուիր, միայն բարձդ կը փոխուի։
Ereeg tsuhkelen pakhduht chee pokhveer, meeayn partsuht guh pokhvee.

35 The coward's mother doesn't cry. (The coward doesn't enter into conflicting situations.)

Վախկոտին մայրը չի լար։
Vakhgodeen mayruh chee lar.

Family

36 The girl who doesn't marry well lives with fantasies (wishes).

Լաւ տեղ չիյնող աղջիկը փափաքներով կ'ապրի։
Lav degh cheeynogh aghcheeguh papaknerov gabree.

37 Everybody has a mother.
(Mourning a mother is universal.)

Ամէն մարդ ալ մայր ունի։
Amen mart al mayr oonee.

38 Beat your wife, you will have beaten seven devils.
(Village superstition; removes evil from wife.)

Ծեծէ կինդ, եօթը սատանայ ծեծած կ'ըլլաս։
Dzedzeh geenuht, yotuh sadana dzedzadz guhllas.

39 Man's worst enemies are a bad wife and cold weather.
(Both are intolerable.)

Մարդուն ամենէն մեծ թշնամիներն են՝ գէշ կինը եւ ցուրտ օդը։
Martoon amenen medz tushnameenern en kesh geenuh yev tsoord otuh.

40 If you have an intelligent son, why do you need money? If you have a foolish son, why do you need money?

Եթէ խելացի տղայ ունիս, դրամը ի՞նչ ընես, եթէ խենթ տղայ ունիս, դրամը ի՞նչ ընես։
Yeteh khelatsee duhgha ooneess, tuhramuh eench uhnes? Yeteh khent duhgha ooneess, tuhramuh eench uhnes?

41 Luck and misfortune are brother and sister, they walk together.

Բախտ եւ անբախտ քոյր եղբայր են, իրարու հետ կը քալեն։
Pakhd yev anpakhd kooyr yekhpayr en, eeraroo hed guh kalen.

42 He's worn out his mother's homespun.
(Wasteful.)

Մօրը մանածը մաշեցուցած է։
Moruh manadzuh mashetsootsadz eh.

43 The man is the head, the wife is the neck.
(Woman controls.)

Մարդը գլուխն է, կինը վիզն է։
Martuh klookhn eh, gueenuh veezn eh.

44 Your child is like a flower, to look upon and be joyful.

Զաւակը ծաղիկ մըն է, վրան կը նայիս կ'ուրախանաս։
Zavaguh dzagheeg muhn eh, vuhran guh nayees goorakhanas.

Family

45 Even if you bring the bride from Baghdad, the son looks like the mother's brother.
(It doesn't matter where one is born, heredity rules.)

Հարսը Պաղտատէն ալ բերես՝ տղան քեռան կը նմանի:
Harsuh Baghdaden al peres deghahn kerahn guh nmanee.

46 Every mother-in-law must put her son-in-law on her head.
(Let every mother-in-law unconditionally support [uphold] her son-in-law.)

Ամէն զոքանչ պիտի իր փեսան գլուխին վրայ դնէ:
Amehn zokanch anbayman beedee eer pesahn klookheen vrah teneh.

47 Daughter, this is the way it is: this is the Lenten month, not the month of the kaka.
(This is the sweet and happy time. Wait until the bad time comes.)

Աղջիկս, այսպէս է, ասի Պահքին ամիսն է, քաքին ամիսը չէ:
Aghcheeguhs, aysbess eh; ahssi Bahkeen ameessn eh, kahkeen ameessuh cheh.

48 You should have left it the way your father built it.
(You should leave well enough alone.)

Հօրդ շինածովը ձգէիր:
Horuht sheenadzovuh tsekeyeer.

49 He hasn't had a bride, he is looking for the bride.
(Confusion.)

Հարս չէ ունեցած, հարսն է կը փնտռէ:
Harss cheh oonetsadz, harssn eh guh puhndreh.

50 Two days would seem like a year, I would miss you.

Երկու օր կ'ըլլայ տարի, ես քեզ կը կարօտնայի:
Yergoo or guhllah daree, yes kez guh garodnayee.

51 "Father, what thing flies the fastest, the moon, the stars, the sun, or the birds?" The father thinks and answers, "Son, time flies ahead the fastest."

«Հայրիկ, ի'նչ բանն ամենէն արագը կը թռի- լուսի՞նը, աստղե՞րը, արե՞ւը կամ թռչունները»: Հայրը կը խորհի ու կը պատասխանէ.- «Տղաս, ժամանակը կ'անցնի ամենէն առաջ»:
"Hayreeg, eench pan amenen arakuh guh turee, looseenuh, asdgheruh, arevuh gam tuhrchoonneruh?" Hayruh guh khorhee oo guh badaskhaneh, "Duhghas, zhamanaguh gantsnee amenen arach."

Լաւութիւնը չարը կը մարէ, բարիքը չարիքին տեղը կը դնէ:

4

God, Good and Evil

"Goodness extinguishes the bad and covers evil with good."

God, Good and Evil

1	A crooked man always speaks crooked.	Սխալ մարդը միշտ սխալ կը խօսի։ *Suhkhal martuh meeshd suhkhal guh khossee.*
2	Did we get rich from eating kaka? (Enough is enough.)	Քա՞ք կերանք, հարստացանք։ *Kak gerank, haruhsdatsank?*
3	Let the sin hang on your neck. (Responsibility for your action.)	Թող մեղքը վիզդ մնայ։ *Togh meghkuh veezuht muhnah.*
4	Atop every evil there is a good thing. In all evil there is something good.	Ամէն չարիքին գլուխ բարիք մը կայ։ Ամէն չարիքի մէջ բարիք մը կայ։ *Amen chareekeen kuhlookh pareek muh gah.* *Amen chareekeen mech pareek muh gah.*
5	The devil moves at night.	Սատանան գիշերը կը շարժի։ *Sadanan keesheruh guh sharzhee.*
6	False friend, hidden enemy.	Սուտ բարեկամ, ներքին թշնամի։ *Sood paregam, nerkeen tuhshnamee.*
7	Pay much attention to the evil talk. (Be aware.)	Գէշ խօսք շատ մտիկ ըրէ։ *Kesh khosk shad muhdeeg uhreh.*
8	Do one, it will return twice.	Մէկ ընեմ, երկու անգամը ետեւէն կու գայ։ *Meg uhnem, yergoo ankamuh yedeven goo kah.*
9	From one to whom a good deed is done you will not see goodness.	Բարիք ստացող մարդէն բարիք չես տեսներ։ *Pareek uhsdatsogh marten pareek ches desner.*
10	You must think good and throw the bad behind you.	Լաւը պիտի խորհիս, գէշը ետեւդ նետես։ *Lavuh beedee khorhees, keshuh yedevuht nedes.*
11	They do two, say they've done three.	Երկու կ'ընեն, երեք ըրին կը խօսին։ *Yergoo guhnen, yerek uhreen guh khoseen.*
12	The do-gooder's beard is kakaed. (Goodness is unappreciated.)	Շատ ընողին մօրուքը կը քաքնեն։ *Shad uhnogheen morookuh guh kaknen.*

13 Pure oil doesn't stay under the water.
(Goodness always surfaces.)

Արդար իւղը ջուրին տակ չի մնար:
Artar yooghuh chooreen dag chee muhnar.

14 Goodness extinguishes the bad and covers evil with good.

Լաւութիւնը չարը կը մարէ, բարիքը չարիքին տեղը կը դնէ:
Lavootyoonuh charuh guh mareh, pareekuh chareekeen deghuh guh tuhneh.

15 If you speak to a good man, he brings goodness; if you speak to a bad man, he brings evil.

Բարի մարդոց հետ խօսիս՝ բարիք կը բերեն, չար մարդոց հետ խօսիս՝ չարիք կը բերեն:
Paree martots hed khosees pareek guh peren; char martots hed khosees chareek guh peren.

16 The goodness done will live even after your death.

Բարի ըրած գործդ մեռնելէդ վերջն ալ կ'ապրի:
Paree uhradz kordzuht mernelet verch al gabree.

17 Does the honest speaker have a hole in his head?
(Honesty is unusual.)

Շիտակ խօսողին թէփէն ծա՞կ կ'ըլլայ:
Sheedag khossogheen tepen dzag guhllah?

18 Every goodness cannot be found in one man.
(Nobody is perfect.)

Ամէն լաւութիւն մէկ մարդու վրայ չ'ըլլար:
Amen lavootyoon meg martoo vrah chuhllar.

19 There are some men, when you spit in their face, they say, "Thank God, the rain came."
(They are unaware, insensitive, shameless.)

Մարդ կայ որ եթէ երեսին վրայ թքնես, կ'ըսէ «Փառք Աստուծոյ, անձրեւ կու գայ»:
Mart gah vor yeteh yereseen vrah tuhknes, guhseh, "Park Asdoodzoh, antsrev goo kah."

20 The Lord makes the saint strong.

Տէրը սուրբը զօրաւոր կ'ընէ:
Deruh soorpuh zoravor guhneh.

21 Let's say good, so all will be good.

Լաւ ըսենք որ լաւ ըլլայ:
Lav uhsenk vor lav uhllah.

22 The orphan's meal is ground by God.
(The orphan is cared for by God.)

Որբին ջաղացքը Աստուած կ'աղայ:
Vorpeen chaghatskuh Asdvadz gaghah.

23 God gives to the giver.

Աստուած տուողին կու տայ:
Asdvadz duhvogheen goo dah.

24 For forty years a sinner, for one year asks forgiveness, the sin will be forgiven. (Forgiveness is always available.)

Քառասուն տարի մեղաւորը, մէկ տարի մեղայ ըսէ, մեղքը կը ներուի:
Karasoon daree meghavoruh, meg daree meghah uhseh, meghkuh guh nervee.

25 May God not allow the one under your foot (an underling) to be over your head.

Աստուած չձգէ որ ոտքիդ տակինը գլուխիդ վրայ ըլլայ:
Asdvadz chuhtsuhkeh vor vodkeet dageenuh kuhlookheet vrah uhllah.

26 The good I do, let God do unto my children.

Ես ընեմ, թող Աստուած ալ պաւակներուս ընէ:
Yes uhnem, togh Asdvadz al zavagneroos uhneh.

27 Fear the man who is not afraid of God or ashamed of his actions.

Աստուծմէ չվախցողէն ու մարդոցմէ չամչցողէն վախցիր:
Asdoodzmeh chuhvakhtsoghen oo martotsmeh chamuhchtsoghen vakhtseer.

28 Let me die without begging for a drop of water; may God not deprive me of my hands and feet.

Կաթիլ մը ջուր չուզած մեռնիմ, Աստուած ձեռքէ ոտքէ չձգէ:
Gateel muh choor choozadz merneem, Asdvadz tserkeh, vodkeh chuhtsuhkeh.

29 An honest man is thrown out of forty villages.

Շիտակ խօսողը քառասուն գիւղէն կը վռնտեն:
Sheedag khosoghuh karasoon kyooghen guh vuhruhnden.

30 Stay away from dwarfs; God has struck them on the head. (That's why they are short.)

Ճուճէներէն հեռու կեցիր, Աստուած իրենց գլխուն զարկած է:
Joojeneren heroo getseer, Asdvadz eerents kuhlkhoon zargadz eh.

31 God turns His face away from a shameless person.

Աստուած երես կը դարձնէ անամօթ մարդէն:
Asdvadz yeresuh guh tartsuhneh anamot marten.

32 God's court is here on earth.

Աստուծոյ դատաստանը հոս է:
Asdoodzoh tadasdanuh hos eh.

33 When God gives, He gives with two hands.

Երբ Աստուած կու տայ, երկու ձեռքով կու տայ:
Yerp Asdvadz goo dah, yergoo tserkov goo dah.

34 God's door is open.

Աստուծոյ դուռը բաց է:
Asdoodzoh tooruh pats eh.

35 I am a saint, he says; the cross comes out of his pocket.
(Hypocrite.)

Սուրբ եմ, կ'ըսէ, խաչը ճէպէն կ'ելլէ:
Soorp em, guhseh, khachuh jeben gelleh.

36 God is with the naive (humble).

Աստուած միամիտին հետ է:
Asdvadz meeyameedeen hed eh.

37 Satan has no work.
(Be careful of temptation.)

Սատանան գործ չունի:
Sadanan kordz choonee.

38 I put my live head under the Gospel.
(Responsibility of commitment.)

Ողջ գլուխս Աւետարանի տակ դրի:
Voghch kuhlookhus Avedareneen dag tuhree.

39 The tombstone of a writer is made of stones thrown at him during his lifetime.
(The courage to speak the truth is shunned while the writer is alive.)

Գրագիրին գերեզմանաքարը, ողջութեան իր հասցէին նետուած քարերով կը շինուի:
Kuhrakeereen kerezmanakaruh, eer hastseyeen nedvadz karerov guh sheenvee.

40 God has a finger to stick in your eye.
(Curse.)

Աստուած մատ ունի որ աչքդ խոթէ:
Asdvadz mad oonee, vor achkuht khoteh.

41 The robber from the robber stole; God saw and was amazed.

Գողը գողէն գողացաւ, Աստուած տեսաւ զարմացաւ:
Koghuh koghen koghatsav, Asdvadz desav zarmatsav.

42 The robber from the robber stole; God saw and observed with joy.

Գողը գողէն գողացաւ, Աստուած տեսաւ ուրախացաւ:
Koghuh koghen koghatsav, Asdvadz desav oorakhatsav.

43 God forbid the loss of your taste buds.
(Wishing you well.)

Աստուած բերնիդ համը չկորսնցնէ։
Asdvadz perneet hamuh chuhgorsuhntsuhneh.

44 May God not allow your right hand to depend on your left hand.
(May God keep you independent.)

Աստուած աջ ձեռքդ ձախ ձեռքիդ չձգէ։
Asdvadz ach tserkuht tsakh tserkeet chuhtsuhkeh.

45 Beat your wife, you will have beaten seven devils.
(Village superstition; removes evil from wife.)

Ծեծէ կինդ, եօթը սատանայ ծեծած կ'ըլլաս։
Dzedzeh geenuht, yotuh sadana dzedzadz guhllas.

46 Sat on the horse, forgot God; got off the horse, forgot the horse.
(Confusion.)

Ձին նստաւ, Աստուած մոռցաւ, ձիէն իջաւ, ձին մոռցաւ։
Tseen nuhsdav, Asdvadz mortsav; tseeyen eechav, tseen mortsav.

47 Let evil take it away.

Չարը տանի։
Charuh danee.

48 God will deal with you.
(God will deal justice.)

Աստուած հաղըդ կու գայ։
Asdvadz haghet goo ka.

49 May he grow up with mother and father.
(A baptismal blessing.)

Հօրով մօրով մեծնայ։
Horov, morov, medzna.

50 Do good, and you don't know in what form it will come back.
(Do good, and it will return to you one way or another.)

Բարիք ըրէ, չես գիտեր ինչ ձեւով ետ կու գայ։
Pareek ereh, chehs keeder eench tsevov yed gooka.

51 Black heart.
(Evil heart; ill wisher.)

Սեւ սիրտ։
Sev seerd.

52 (He) has evil intent.

Գէշ նպատակ ունի։
Kesh nbadag oonee.

53 Every man has a pain, every tree has a worm.

Ամէն մարդ ցաւ ունի, ամէն ծառ որդ ունի։
Amen mart tsav oonee, amen dzar vort oonee.

54 Let the days be yours.
(Wishing long life. Usually said to a person when speaking of the death of another.)

Օրերը քեզի։
Oreruh kezee.

55 May the writer (the angel of death) take him.

Գրողը տանի։
Kroghuh dahnee.

56 The good takes away the bad.
(Goodness prevails.)

Բարին չարը կը տանի։
Pareen charuh guh dahnee.

57 Right now, I am fine; let God think about tomorrow.
(I leave the future to God.)

Հիմակու հիմա լաւ եմ։ Վաղուան մասին թող Աստուած մտածէ։
Heemagoo heema lav em; vaghvahn mahsseen togh Asdvadz medadzeh.

58 May God illuminate his soul.
(May God have mercy on his soul.)

Աստուած հոգին լուսաւորէ։
Asdvadz hokeen loossavoreh.

59 The guest is God's messenger.
(This is said to a guest upon his arrival.)

Հիւրը Աստուածին (Աստուծոյ) պատգամաւորն է։
Hyuruh Asdvadzeen (Asdoodzo) badkamavorn eh.

60 May your sun increase.
(May you be blessed.)

Արեւդ շատնայ։
Arevuht shahdna.

61 May you see their future.
(Wishing future blessings.)

Խէրը տեսնաս։
Kheruh dessnass.

62 God gives a man one thousand and one encumbrances so he will not be preoccupied with death.

Աստուած մարդուն հազար ու մէկ զբաղում կու տայ որ մահուան վրայ չմտածէ։
Asdvadz martoon hazar oo meg zpaghoom goo da vor mahvan vra chmdadzeh.

Առողջ միտք, առողջ մարմինին:

5

Health

"Healthy mind, healthy body."

Health

1	He who cannot control his eating has no control over his doings.	Ան որ կերածը չի կրնար կառավարել, ըրածը հէչ չի կրնար կառավարել։ *An vor geradzuh chee guhrnar garavarel, uhradzuh hech chee guhrnar garavarel.*
2	When ill, you will eat tasteless soup. (The cure is bitter.)	Հիւանդ ես, պիտի ուտես մալէզ ապուր։ *Heevant es, beedee oodes malez aboor.*
3	The bad sore will heal, the bad word remains.	Գէշ եարան կ'աղէկնայ, գէշ խօսքը կը մնայ։ *Kesh yaran gaghegnah, kesh khoskuh guh muhnah.*
4	Sickness becomes a needle, enters the body, becomes a camel, and won't leave.	Հիւանդութիւնը ասեղ կ'ըլլայ՝ կը մտնէ, ուղտ կ'ըլլայ՝ չ'ելլեր։ *Heevantootyoonuh asegh guhllah, guh muhdneh, ooghd guhllah, cheller.*
5	Healthy mind, healthy body.	Առողջ միտք, առողջ մարմինին։ *Aroghch meedk, aroghch marmeeneen.*
6	Eat and be satisfied.	Կե՛ր եւ գոհացիր։ *Ger yev kohatseer.*
7	I haven't eaten onion, so my stomach can't hurt. (There is no fear with prevention.)	Սոխ չեմ կերած որ փորս ցաւի։ *Sokh chem geradz vor poruhs tsavee.*
8	Enters by the *ghantar* (110 pounds) and comes out by the *direm* (one ounce). (Sickness comes in strong, but healing comes slowly.)	Ներս կը մտնէ ղանթարով, դուրս կ'ելլէ տիրէմով։ *Nerss guh muhdneh ghantarov, toors guelleh diremov.*
9	The healthy one dies, the sick becomes alive. (Life is a paradox.)	Սաղը (առողջը) կը մեռնի՝ հիւանդը կ'ողջնայ։ *Saghuh (aroghchuh) guh mernee, heevantuh guh voghchanna.*

10 He drained the blood. (He drained the emotions.)	Արիւն քամեց։ *Aryun kahmets.*
11 When afflicted with stress (fright, terror), it affects the weakest part of the body.	Սոսկումը ունենաս, նապիկ տեղը կը բռնէ։ *Sosgoomuh oonenahs, nahzeeg deghuh guh perneh.*
12 Whatever your stomach desires, eat; otherwise it becomes a negative to your body.	Ինչ որ 'միտէ'դ կը քաշէ, կե՛ր, թէ ոչ հակառակ կ'ըլլայ մարմինիդ։ *Eench vohr meedeht guh kahsheh, guehr, teh voch hagarag guhlla marmeeneet.*
13 The heart is willing, the body is weak.	Հոգին յօժար է, մարմինը տկար է։ *Hokeen hojar eh, marmeenuh dgar eh.*

Հոն ուր ձի չկայ, էշն ալ յարգ ունի։

6

Living Creatures

"Where there is no horse, the donkey has respect."

1 One frightened by wolves will not keep sheep.

Գայլէն վախցողը ոչխար չի պահեր:
Kaylen vakhtsoghuh vochkhar chee baher.

2 Our sick sheep is more desirable than anyone's healthy wolf.

Մեր հիւանդ ոչխարը աւելի լաւ է քան թէ ուրիշին առողջ գայլը:
Mer heevant vochkharuh avelee lav eh, kan teh ooreesheen arokhch kayluh.

3 The Bible was read to the wolf; he said, "Finish, the sheep will get away."

Գայլին գլխուն Աւետարան կը կարդան, կ'ըսէ «Լմնցո՛ւր, ոչխարը պիտի փախի»:
Kayleen kuhlkhoon Avedaran guh gartan, guhseh, "Luhmuhntsoor, vochkharuh beedee pakhee."

4 The dead donkey doesn't fear the wolf.

Մեռած էշը գայլէն չի վախնար:
Meradz eshuh kaylen chee vakhnar.

5 When the wolf ages, dogs make fun of it.

Գայլը եթէ ծերանայ, շուներուն ծաղրանք կ'ըլլայ:
Kayluh yeteh dzeranah, shooneroon dzaghrank guhllah.

6 A sweet tongue will draw the snake from the hole.

Անուշ լեզուն օձը ծակէն կը հանէ:
Anoosh lezoon otsuh dzagen guh haneh.

7 Let the snake who doesn't touch me live a thousand years.

Ինծի չդպած օձը թող հազար տարի ապրի:
Eendzee chuhtuhbadz otsuh togh hazar daree abree.

8 The snake changes its skin, but it's the same snake.

Օձը իր կաշին կը փոխէ, բայց միեւնոյն օձն է:
Otsuh eer gasheen guh pokheh, paytz meeyevnooyn otsn eh.

9 The snake, which is a snake, when it drinks water looks up (to heaven). (Gratitude.)

Օձը որ օձ է, երբ ջուր խմէ վեր կը նայի:
Otsuh vor ots eh, yerp choor khuhmeh ver guh nayee.

10 When the rich man ate snake, they said it was medicine, but when the poor man ate it, they said he was hungry.	Հարուստը օձ կերաւ, ըսին դեղ է, իսկ երբ չունեցողը կերաւ՝ ըսին անօթի է: *Haroosduh ots gerav, uhsen tegh eh, eesg yerp choonetsoghuh gerav, uhsen anotee eh.*
11 He who falls into the sea will wrap around a snake. (Desperation.)	Ծովը ինկողը օձին կը փաթթուի: Dzovn eengoghuh otseen guh pattuhvee.
12 The snake's most disliked weed grows through its door's hole. (Unpleasant happening.)	Օձին չսիրած խոտը դուռին ծակէն կը բուսնի: *Otseen chuhseeradz khoduh tooreen dzagen guh poosnee.*
13 Mice also eat salad. (Don't be surprised.)	Մուկերն ալ սալաթա կ'ուտեն: *Moogern al salatah gooden.*
14 The cat, which is a cat, will run after the mouse. (Natural instinct.)	Կատուն որ կատու է, մուկին ետեւէն կը վազէ: *Gadoon vor gadoo eh, moogeen yedeven guh vazeh.*
15 The mouse and the fish in one pan, which will you eat? (Neither is edible.)	Մուկը, ձուկը մէկ թաւա, ո՞րը կ'ուտես: *Mooguh, tsooguh meg tavah, voruh goodes?*
16 The one who fell from the horse didn't die, but the one who fell from the donkey did.	Ձիուն վրայէն ինկողը չէ մեռած, բայց էշին վրայէն ինկողը մեռեր է: *Tseeyoon vrayen eengoghuh cheh meradz, payts esheen vrayen eengoghuh merer eh.*
17 Where there is no horse, the donkey has respect.	Հոն ուր ձի չկայ, էշն ալ յարգ ունի: *Hon oor tsee chuhgah, eshn al hark oonee.*
18 The donkey works, the horse gets the glory.	Էշը կը գործէ, ձին կը վայելէ: *Eshuh guh kordzeh, tseen guh vayeleh.*

19 The horse was whipped, did his teeth fall out?
(Exaggeration.)

Ձին զարկին, ակռա՞ն ինկաւ:
Tseen zargeen, agran eengav?

20 The fish dies through its mouth.
(Gossip hurts.)

Ձուկը բերնէն կը մեռնի:
Tsooguh pernen guh mernee.

21 The fish rotted from the head.
(Corruption starts from the top.)

Ձուկը գլուխէն հոտեր է:
Tsooguh kuhlookhen hoder eh.

22 It was asked of the fish, "What news do you have from the sea?" The fish said, "I have much to say, but my mouth is full of water."
(Ask the person who knows.)

Ձուկին հարցուցին, «Ծովէն ի՞նչ լուր», ըսաւ «Շատ բան ունիմ ըսելիք, բայց բերանս ջուրով լեցուն է»:
Tsoogeen hartsootseen, "Dzoven eench loor?" Uhsav "Shad pan ooneem uhseleek, payts peranuhs choorov letsoon eh."

23 Do good, throw it into the sea. If the one that receives doesn't appreciate it, the fish will.
(Someone benefits.)

Բարիք ըրէ. ծովը նետէ, եթէ առնողը չի գիտնար՝ ձուկը կը գիտնայ:
Pareek muh uhreh, dzovuh nedeh; yeteh arnoghuh chee keednar, tsooguh guh keednah.

24 Throw your bread into the sea. If the wave doesn't notice, the fish will.
(Someone benefits.)

Հացդ ծովը նետէ, ալիքը չի գիտնայ՝ ձուկը կը գիտնայ:
Hatsuht dzovuh nedeh, aleekuh chee keednah, tsooguh guh keednah.

25 What does the jackass know about almonds?
(Unaware; ignorant.)

Էշը ի՞նչ գիտէ նուշը ինչ է:
Eshuh eench keedeh nooshuh eench eh?

26 What does the jackass know about fruit compote?
(Unaware.)

Էշը խոշափէն ի՞նչ կը հասկնայ:
Eshuh khoshapen eench guh hasguhnah?

27 What does a donkey know about taste when he goes and eats seeded thorns?

Էշն ի՞նչ գիտէ բերնին ուշը, կ'երթայ կ'ուտէ կուտոտ փուշը:
Eshn eench keedeh perneen ooshuh, gertah goodeh goodod pooshuh.

28 Every donkey has four legs.
(So what's new?)

Ամէն էշ չորս ոտք ունի:
Amen esh chors vodk oonee.

29 The ass's tail was cut short; some said it was short, some said it was long.
(Selective observation.)

Էշուն պոչը կտրեցին, որը կ'ըսէ կարճ է, որը կ'ըսէ երկար է:
Eshoon bochuh guhdretseen, voruh guhseh garj eh, voruh guhseh yergar eh.

30 They dye the donkey, and they sell it as a horse.
(Deception.)

Էշը կը ներկեն, ձիու տեղ կը ծախեն:
Eshuh guh nergen, tseeyoo degh guh dzakhen.

31 I left the large donkey at the stable.
(Oversight.)

Մեծ էշը ախոռը թողուցի:
Medz eshuh akhoruh toghootsee.

32 He is searching for his jackass while sitting on it.

Իշուն վրայ նստեր է, էշ կը փնտռէ:
Eeshoon vuhrah nuhsder eh, esh guh puhndreh.

33 The donkey, which is a donkey, will bow its head when the church bell chimes.

Էշը որ էշ է, զանգակը եթէ չալէ կը խոնարհի:
Eshuh vor esh eh, zankaguh yeteh chaleh, guh khonarhee.

34 Even if you were born a jackass, you would understand.
(Ignorance is no excuse.)

Էշ կը ծնիս, կը հասկնաս:
Esh guh dzuhnees, guh hasguhnas.

35 What should the dead donkey fear?
(Death has no reaction.)

Մեռած էշը ինչէ՞ն կը վախնայ:
Meradz eshuh eenchen guh vakhnah?

36 Let them call me bad, but don't call me a jackass.
(Don't let them belittle my goodness.)

Թող գէշ ըսեն, թող էշ չըսեն:
Togh kesh uhssehn, togh esh chuhssen.

37 The jackass plays the piano.
(Surprise.)

Էշը դաշնակ կը նուագէ:
Eshuh tashnag guh nuhvakeh.

38 The donkey, which is a donkey, falls in the mud only once.

Էշը որ էշ է, ցեխին մէջ միայն մէկ անգամ կ'իյնայ:
Eshuh vor esh eh, tsekheen mech meeayn meg ankam geeynah.

39 They went with the donkey's saddle, they came out with the donkey's saddle. (Nothing changes.)

Էշին փալանով կ'երթան, էշին փալանով դուրս կ'ելլեն:
Esheen palanov gertan; esheen palanov toors gellen.

40 If you tie a man and a donkey together, the donkey can't become a man, but the man can become a jackass.

Եթէ մարդն ու էշը իրարու քով կապես, էշը մարդ չի կրնար ըլլալ, բայց մարդը էշ կրնայ ըլլալ:
Yeteh martn oo eshuh eeraroo kov gabes, eshuh mart chee guhrnar uhllal, payts martuh esh guhrnah uhllal.

41 Being a jackass, treated badly. (Being stupid, became a victim.)

Էշ ըլլալուս գէշ կ'ըլլամ:
Esh uhllaloos kesh guhllam.

42 Tie a jackass next to a jackass, either the glory or the manner will take. (Influence.)

Էշը որ էշին քով կապես, կամ փառքէն կ'առնէ կամ վարքէն:
Eshuh vor esheen kov gabes, gam parken garneh gam varken.

43 Call a man a jackass for ten days, he will become one. (Self-fulfilling prophecy.)

Մարդը տասը օր էշ կանչես, էշ կ'ըլլայ:
Martuh dasuh or esh ganches, esh guhllah.

44 A dog, to another dog, doesn't say, "You are a dog." (A sinner doesn't attack another sinner.)

Շունը շան շուն չ'ըսեր:
Shoonuh shanuh shoon chuhser.

45 A dog will not eat a dog's carcass. (Doesn't attack its own kind.)

Շունը շան միս չ'ուտեր:
Shoonuh shan meesuh chooder.

46 The dog doesn't recognize his master. (Confusion.)

Շունը տէրը չի ճանչնար:
Shoonuh deruh chee janchnar.

47 When the dog's need comes, he dirties on the enemy's doorstep. (Instinct comes before respect.)

Երբ շանը ճէլէն գայ, թշնամուն դուռը կ'աղտոտէ:
Yerp shanuh ejelen kah, tshnamoon tooruh gaghdodeh.

48 The sugar fell into the dog's mouth.
(Undeserved luck.)

Շաքարը շան բերանն ինկեր է:
Shakaruh shan perann eenger eh.

49 The dog commands the dog, and the tail commands it.
(Passing the buck.)

Շունը շունին կը հրամայէ, պոչն ալ շունին կը հրամայէ:
Shoonuh shooneen guh huhramayeh, bochn al shooneen guh huhramayeh.

50 Don't hope for whiteness; snow is white, too, but the dogs dirty it.
(Don't be fooled.)

Ճերմակութեան մի՛ փափաքիր, ձիւնն ալ ճերմակ է, շուները վրան կ'աղտոտեն:
Jermagootyan mee papakeer, tsyoonn al jermag eh, shooneruh vran gaghdoden.

51 Can't make leather from a dog's skin.
(Limitations on usage.)

Շունին մորթէն կաշի չ'ելլեր:
Shooneen morten gashee chuhllar.

52 The red cow was killed, but its skin remained red.
(Don't be deceived; things are not what they seem.)

Կարմիր կովը մորթեր են, նորէն մորթը կարմիր է:
Garmeer govuh morter en, noren mortuh garmeer eh.

53 A cow, like a cow, gives milk, later strikes with her tail and spills it.
(Good deed overturned.)

Կովը կովի պէս կաթը կու տայ, վերջը պոչով կը զարնէ ու կը թափէ:
Govuh govee bes gatuh goo dah, verchuh bochov guh zarneh oo guh tapeh.

54 One Armenian eats one chicken, two Armenians eat two chickens, three Armenians eat each other.

Մէկ հայը մէկ հաւ կ'ուտէ, երկու հայերը երկու հաւ կ'ուտեն, երեք հայերը զիրար կ'ուտեն:
Meg hayuh meg hav goodeh, yergoo hayeruh yergoo hav gooden, yerek hayeruh zeerar gooden.

55 On rainy days there are many givers of water to the hens.
(Irony: when there is a real need, no one is available.)

Անձրեւոտ օրը հաւերուն ջուր տուող շատ կ'ըլլայ:
Antsrevod oruh haveroon choor duhvogh shad guhllah.

56 The rooster who crows out of season will lose his neck.

Ժամանակէն դուրս կանչած խորոզի վիզը կը կտրեն:
Zhamanagen toors ganchadz khorozeen veezuh guh guhdren.

57 The chicken fluttered, did the wall cave in? (Exaggeration.)

Հաւը թռաւ, պա՞տը փլաւ:
Havuh tuhrav, baduh puhlav?

58 The chicken that lays eggs cackles much. (Boastful.)

Ածան հաւը շատ կը կռկռայ:
Adzan havuh shad guh guhrguhrah.

59 By the time the hen is done, the grain will start to sprout. (Procrastination; laziness.)

Հաւը ըրած, կուտը բուսած:
Hahvuh uhradz, gooduh poosadz.

60 Even the cooked chicken would laugh at you.

Եփած հաւը վրադ կը խնդայ:
Yepadz havuh vraht guh khuhntah.

61 The hen, which is a hen, when drinking water looks up (to heaven). (Gratitude.)

Հաւը որ հաւ է, ջուր խմէ նէ՝ վեր կը նայի:
Havuh vor hav eh, choor khuhmen neh, ver guh nayee.

62 What the hen won't eat… (Glutton; will eat anything in sight.)

Հաւուն չկերածը…
Havoon chuhgeradzuh.

63 The neighbor's wife looks like a bride, the neighbor's hen looks like a goose. (Everything looks better from afar.)

Դրացիին կինը հարս կ'երեւայ, դրացիին հաւն ալ ղազ կ'երեւայ:
Tuhratseeyeen geenuh hars gerevah, tuhratseeyeen havn al ghaz gerevah.

64 Raise the black crow, so it will gouge your eye out. (Do good, and get evil in return.)

Սեւ ղուշը մեծցուր որ աչքդ փորէ:
Sev ghooshuh medztsoor vor achkuht poreh.

65 Ant or bird without a nose (to direct) can't fly. (Knowledge is necessary.)

Մրջիւն, թռչուն քիթերսուզ չեն թռիր:
Muhrchyoon, turhchoon keetersooz chen tuhreer.

66 You can't catch a bird with one hand.

Մէկ ձեռքով թռչուն չի բռնուիր:
Meg tserkov tuhrchoon chee puhrnuhveer.

67 The bird lands on a branch, that branch saves that bird.
(Help in time of need. Genocide reference.)

Թռչունը տալին վրայ իջնայ, այն տալը այն թռչունը կ’ապատէ։
Tuhrchoonuh daleen vrah eechnah, ayn daluh ayn tuhrchoonuh gazadeh.

68 If you’re afraid of birds, you can’t plant wheat.

Թռչունէն եթէ վախնաս, ցորեն չես ցաներ։
Tuhrchoonen yeteh vakhnas, tsoren ches tsaner.

69 When drinking water, the crow looks upward (to heaven).
(Gratitude.)

Ղուշը ջուր խմէ նէ, երվան կը նայի։
Ghooshuh choor khuhmeh neh, yervan guh nayee.

70 The goat’s least savored weed grows under his nose.
(Unpleasant or unexpected happening.)

Այծին չսիրած խոտը քիթին տակը կը բուսնի։
Aydzeen chuhseeradz khoduh keeteen daguh guh poosnee.

71 The animal knows by smelling, man by talking.
(Instinct.)

Կենդանին հոտուըտալով կը գիտնայ, մարդը՝ խօսելով։
Gentaneen hodvuhdalov guh keednah, martuh khoselov.

72 The camel can’t see his hump.
(Doesn’t recognize his own fault.)

Ուղտը սապատը չի տեսներ։
Ooghduh eer sabaduh chee desner.

73 It was asked of the camel, “Why is your neck crooked?” The camel replied, “What part of me is straight, that my neck should be, too?”

Ուղտին ըսեր են, «Ինչո՞ւ վիզդ ծուռ է», ուղտը ըսեր է, «Իմ որտե՞ղս շիտակ է որ, վիզս ալ շիտակ ըլլայ»։
Ooghdeen uhser en, “Eenchoo veezuht dzoor eh?” Ooghduh uhser eh, “Eem vordeghuhs sheedag eh, vor veezuhs al sheedag uhllah?”

74 The donkey brings the hay, but the horse is the one who eats it.
(Undeserved reward.)

Էշը կը տանի յարդը, ձին է ուտողը։
Eshuh guh danee hartuh, tseen eh oodoghuh.

75 Only the horse can resist another horse’s kick.
(Within family, don’t heed a hurt.)

Ձիու աքացիին ձին կը դիմանայ միայն։
Tseeyoo akatseeyeen tseen guh teemana meeayn.

76 The sting of disdain can pierce even the turtle's shell.

Արհամարհանքին խայթոցը կրնայ ծակել կրիային պատեանն անգամ:
Arhamarankeen khaytotsuh guhrnah dzagel guhryayeen badyann ankam.

77 The largest portion is eaten by the bear.
(Power overwhelms.)

Ամենէն խոշորը արջը կ'ուտէ:
Amenen khoshoruh archuh goodeh.

78 The butterfly went up the tree, what is and what isn't (everything) dropped down.
(Impossible situation.)

Թիթեռնիկը ծառ է ելեր, ինչ կայ չի կայ վար է թափեր:
Teeterneeguh dzar eh yeler, eench gah chee gah var eh taper.

79 Sat on the horse, forgot God; got off the horse, forgot the horse.
(Confusion.)

Ձին նստաւ, Աստուած մոռցաւ, ձիէն իջաւ՝ ձին մոռցաւ:
Tseen nuhsdav, Asdvadz mortsav, tseeyen eechav, tseen mortsav.

80 The fly isn't dirty, but when it falls in the water, it spoils your appetite.

Ճանճը փիս չէ, բայց ջուրին մէջ ախորժակ կ'աւրէ:
Janjuh pees cheh, paytz chooreen mech eeynah akhorzhag gavreh.

81 Under the lamb's skin is a wolf.
(Be aware; don't be fooled.)

Գառնուկի մորթին տակ գայլ է:
Karnoogee morteen dag kayl eh.

82 It was asked of the cat, "Did your dirt (excrement) come out?" The cat buried it.
(Avoids or covers the truth.)

Կատուին ըսած են, «Աղտոտութի՛ւնդ ելա՞ւ». կատուն թաղած է աղտոտութիւնը:
Gadooyeen uhsadz en, "Aghdodootyoonuht yelav?" Gadoon taghadz eh aghdodootyoonuh.

83 Crocodile tears are shed.
(False tears are shed.)

Կոկորդիլոսի արցունք կը թափէ:
Gogorteelosee artsoonk guh tapeh.

84 Every sheep is hung by its feet.
(Right way to do things.)

Ամէն ոչխար իր ոտքէն կը կախեն:
Amen vochkhar eer vodken guh gakhen.

85 There is a fly on the wall.
(Someone's listening.)

Պատը ճանճ կայ:
Bahduh janj gah.

86 The cat can't reach the liver, so he says it's spoiled.
(Sour grapes.)

Կատուն ճիկերին չի հասնիր, հոտած է կ'ըսէ:
Gadoon jeegereen chee hasneer, hodadz eh guhseh.

87 Lice got bloodied.
(Got rich.)

Ոջիլը արիւնեցաւ:
Vocheeluh aryoonetsav.

88 Whatever the chicken is, expect the same from its home.

Հաւը ի՛նչ է որ տունն ինչ ըլլայ:
Havuh eench eh vor doonn eench uhllah.

89 Dog and cat.
(Argumentative.)

Շուն ու կատու:
Shoon oo gadoo.

90 Don't drop pearls in front of swine.

Խոզերուն առջեւ մարգարիտ մի՛ նետեր:
Khozeroon archev markareed mee neder.

91 The bird an ant, the ant a bird.
(Confusion.)

Թռչունը՝ մրջիւն, մրջիւնը՝ թռչուն:
Turchoonuh muhrchyoon, muhrchyoonuh tuhrchoon.

92 In every heart there is a lion.

Ամէն սրտի մէջ առիւծ մը կայ:
Amen suhrdee mech aryoods muh gah.

93 Pretending to be a fool, he ate the monastery's chickens.
(Deception; taking advantage.)

Սուտ խենթ եղած է, վանքի հաւերը կ'ուտէ:
Sood khent yeghadz eh, vankee haveruh goodeh.

94 Sickness becomes a needle, enters the body, becomes a camel, and won't leave.

Հիւանդութիւնը ասեղ կ'ըլլայ՝ կը մտնէ, ուղտ կ'ըլլայ՝ չ'ելլեր:
Heevantootyoonuh asegh guhllah, guh muhdneh, ooghd guhllah, cheller.

95 Don't send an old man for a donkey or a young man for a bride.
(Be aware of foolish judgment.)

Ծեր մարդ մի՛ ղրկեր՝ էշի համար, երիտասարդ մի՛ ղրկեր հարսի համար:
Dzer mart mee ghuhrger eshee hamar, yereedasart mee ghuhrger harsee hamar.

96 The thief who steals eggs will also steal chickens.

Հաւկիթին գողը հաւ ալ կը գողնայ:
Havgeeteen koghuh hav al guh koghnah.

97 Everyone thinks his worries are as large as a camel.

Ամէն մարդ կը խորհի իր տէրտը ուղտի չափ խոշոր է:
Amen mart guh khorhee eer derduh ooghdee chap khoshor eh.

98 He ate the donkey, but he was troubled by the tail.
(Finished the big job but got troubled by the last small portion.)

Էշը կերաւ, պոչէն խռովաւ:
Eshuh gerav, bochen khuhrovav.

99 He makes his donkey walk.
(Pushing his own agenda.)

Իր էշը կը քալեցնէ:
Eer eshuh guh kaletseneh.

100 Head of jackass.
(Stubborn.)

Էշու գլուխ:
Eshoo klookh.

101 He is looking for the donkey, while he is sitting on the donkey.
(Cannot see beyond his nose.)

Էշը կը փնտռէ, էշին վրայ նստեր է:
Eshuh guh pendreh, esheen vrah nesder eh.

102 Once the nightingale leaves the cage, he will not return.
(Lost opportunity.)

Պուլպուլը եթէ վանդակէն փախի ետ չի վերադառնար:
Boolbooluh yeteh vantaguen pakhee, yed chee veratarnar.

103 The dog's kaka doesn't remain under the snow.
(Truth will always be exposed.)

Շունին քաքը ձիւնին տակը չի մնար:
Shooneen kakuh tsyuneen dahguh chee menar.

104 What is there, what isn't there? There is a camel's tail.
(What's new? Nothing. The camel has no tail.)

Ի՞նչ կայ չկայ. տէվէին պոչը կայ:
Eench ga chega. Deveyeen bochuh gah.

105 We forgot the big donkey.
(We forgot the most important.)

Էշուն մեծը մոռցանք:
Eshoon medzuh mohrtsank.

106 As big as a donkey.
(Huge.)

Էշու չափ:
Eshoo chahp.

107 The snake, which is a snake, measures the soil he eats.
(One who is cheap measures everything. Or: Discernment, wise as a serpent.)

Օձը որ օձ է խնայողաբար հողը կ'ուտէ:
Otsuh vor ots eh khuhnayoghapar hoghuh goodeh.

Ջուրը չտեսած փէշերը կը սօթտէ:

7

Morality and Wisdom

"Before seeing the water, she gathers her skirt."

1 He who humbles himself shall be exalted.

Խոնարհողը կը բարձրանայ:
Khonarhoghuh guh patsranah.

2 Let the writer (the angel of death) eat, let the mother eat, let her eat half of the eggs of her seven children.
(It's not what it seems.)

Գրող ուտէ, մայրը ուտէ, եօթը զաւակին հաւկիթին կէս-կէս ուտէ:
Kuhrogh oodeh, mayruh oodeh, yotuh zavagueen havgeeteen ges-ges oodeh.

3 I drink milk drop by drop, I eat your flesh with zest.
(I gossip about you with pleasure.)

Պատիկ-պատիկ կաթ խմեմ, դոփիկ-դոփիկ միսդ ուտեմ:
Badeeg-badeeg gat khuhmem, topeeg-topeeg meesuht oodem.

4 The orphan poured water on his head, heaven and earth darkened.
(Unfortunate.)

Որբը գլուխը ջուր դրեր է, երկինք եւ գետին մթներ են:
Vorpuh kuhlookhuh choor tuhrer eh, yergeenk yev kedeen mutner en.

5 First fortune is a golden crown.
(Unexpected luck.)

Առաջին բախտը ոսկէ թագդ է:
Aracheen pakhduh vosgeh takuht eh.

6 You may be asleep, but your luck is awake.

Դուն քուն, բախտդ արթուն:
Toon koon, pakhduht artoon.

7 The robber from the robber stole; God saw and was amazed.

Գողը գողէն գողացաւ, Աստուած տեսաւ զարմացաւ:
Koghuh koghen koghatsav, Asdvadz desav zarmatsav.

8 What can a dark-skinned person do with soap? What can a fool do with advice?

Էսմերը սապոնը ի՞նչ ընէ, խեւը խրատն ի՞նչ ընէ:
Esmeruh sabonuh eench uhneh, khevuh khuhradn eench uhneh?

9 Whatever you plant, that's what you will reap.

Ինչ որ ցանես, ան կը հնձես:
Eench vor tsanehs, ayn guh huhntses.

10 Crying the sin and paying the debt.
(Repentance for sin and repayment for debt.)

Մեղքը լալով, պարտքը տալով:
Mekhkuh lalov, bardkuh dalov.

11 Citizenship is enjoyable, if you have money in your hands.	Քաղաքացիութիւնը համ ունի, երբ որ ձեռքդ դրամ ունիս։ *Kaghakatzeeyootyoonuh ham oonee, yerp vor tserkuht tuhram oonees.*
12 I say *pahn* (thing), you say *tahn* (yogurt drink). (We don't communicate.)	Ես բան կ'ըսեմ, դուն թան կ'ըսես։ *Yes pahn guhsem, toon tahn guhses.*
13 When you get old, you will understand and respect the aged.	Երբ ծերանաս, ծերին յարգը կ'իմանաս։ *Yerp dzeranas, dzereen harkuh geemanas.*
14 In front, a mirror; in back, a razor. (Hypocrisy.)	Առջեւը՝ հայելի, ետեւը՝ ածելի։ *Archevuh hayelee, yedevuh adzelee.*
15 Very sweet, but underneath is a thorn.	Շատ անուշ է, բայց տակը փուշ է։ *Shad anoosh eh, payts daguh poosh eh.*
16 It's easy to be generous with other people's money.	Դիւրին է ուրիշի դրամով առատ ըլլալ։ *Tyooreen eh ooreesheen tuhramov arad uhllal.*
17 With joyfulness the hair grows long, with sadness the fingernails. (Joy brings growth, sadness brings neglect.)	Ուրախութենէն մազը կ'երկարի, տխրութենէն՝ եղունգը։ *Oorakhootenen mazuh gergaree, duhkhrootenen yeghoonkuh.*
18 Go die, come (back), then I will love you. (Unappreciated while alive.)	Գնա մեռիր, եկուր սիրեմ։ *Kuhnah mereer, yegoor seerem.*
19 As much as the iron is worked, that much more it will shine.	Երկաթը որչափ որ գործէ, այնքան կը փայլի։ Yergatuh vorchap vor kordzeh, aynkan guh paylee.
20 He who falls or trips himself will not cry.	Ինքն իրեն ինկողը չի լար։ *Eenkn eeren eengoghuh chee lar.*

21 Given with the spoon, taken out with the handle.
(Reminder of kindness forfeits the good deed.)

Դգալով կու տան, կոթով կը հանեն։
Tuhkalov goo dan, gotov guh hanen.

22 If you hold his nose, will his spirit come out?
(Exaggerated outcome.)

Քիթը բռնես, հոգի՞ն կ’ելլէ։
Keetuh puhrnes, hokeen gelleh?

23 I’ll say one, you understand it as two.
(I’m giving you a hint.)

Ես մէկ ըսեմ, դուն երկու հասկցիր։
Yes meg uhsem, toon yergoo hasguhtseer.

24 One who digs the ditch falls in the ditch.
(Evil action befalls the perpetrator.)

Փոսը փորողը փոսը կ’իյնայ։
Posuhs poroghuh, posuh geeynah.

25 Run, run, but you will never arrive.
(No goals.)

Վազես, վազես չես հասնիր։
Vazes, vazes ches hasneer.

26 Enters through a needle hole, but can’t get through a packing needle hole.
(Difficult situation.)

Ասեղին ծակէն կը մտնէ, մախաթին ծակէն չ’ելլեր։
Asegheen dzagen guh muhdneh, makhateen dzagen cheller.

27 Hangs a tail on everyone.
(Criticism, judgment.)

Ամէն մարդու վրայ պոչ մը կը կախէ։
Amen martoo vuhrah boch muh guh gakheh.

28 Hope remained in the stomach.
(Unfulfilled.)

Փափաքը փորը մնաց։
Papakuh poruh muhnats.

29 From every head comes a sound.
(Different opinions.)

Ամէն գլուխէն ձայն մը կ’ելլէ։
Amen kuhlookhen tsayn muh gelleh.

30 Even if gold falls in the mud, it is still gold.

Ոսկին, եթէ չամուրին մէջ ալ իյնայ, նորէն ոսկի է։
Vosgeen, yeteh chamooreen mech al eeynah, noren vosgee eh.

31 Upon falling to the ground, gold doesn’t become tin.

Ոսկին գետին իյնալով թիթեղ չ’ըլլար։
Vosgeen kedeen eeynalov teetegh chuhllar.

32	By what measure you weigh, the same measure will be dealt to you.	Ինչ չափով որ կը կշռես, նոյն չափով կը կշռուիս։ *Eench chapov vor guhshres, nooyn chapov guh guhshruhvees.*
33	When the pot overboils, the heat overflows on its own head. (Unwise decisions have consequences.)	Պտուկը. եթէ եփի, կրակը իր գլխուն վրայ կը լեցուի։ *Buhdooguh, yeteh yepee, guhraguh eer kulkhoon vrah guh letsvee.*
34	There is a fly on the wall. (Someone's listening.)	Պատը ճանճ կայ։ *Baduh janj gah.*
35	Today's idle chatter tomorrow will bring danger.	Այսօրուան պօշ խօսիլը վաղուան վնաս կու տայ։ *Aysorvan bosh khoseeluh vaghvan vuhnas goo dah.*
36	As much as you stir, the smell will increase. (Gossip.)	Որչափ խառնես, հոտը կ'ելլէ։ *Vorchap kharnes, hoduh gelleh.*
37	The tongue has no bone. (The tongue is loose. Gossip.)	Լեզուն ոսկոր չունի։ *Lezoon vosgor choonee.*
38	Hair has grown on my tongue. (I nagged but to no avail.)	Լեզուիս վրայ մազ բուսաւ։ *Lezvees vrah maz poosav.*
39	Every man says his sour yogurt is sweet. (Not truthful, boastful.)	Ամէն մարդ կ'ըսէ թանս անուշ է։ *Amen mart guhseh tahnus anoosh eh.*
40	Whatever I say, write it on ice. (What I say is meaningless.)	Ինչ որ ըսեմ, սառին վրայ գրէ։ *Eench vor uhsem, sareen vuhrah kuhreh.*
41	Until the lie is revealed, truth cannot exist.	Սուտը մինչեւ չյայտնուի, շիտակին տեղ չկայ։ *Sooduh meenchev chuhhaydnuhvee sheedageen degh chee gah.*

42 There is no room for him who speaks the truth.
(Truthfulness is not honored.)

Շիտակ խօսողին տեղ չկայ։
Sheedag khosogheen degh chee gah.

43 How can I question honest speech?

Շիտակ խօսքին ի՞նչ ըսեմ։
Sheedag khoskeen eench uhsem?

44 Can't wash blood away with blood.
(No-win situation.)

Արիւնը արիւնով չի լուացուիր։
Aryoonuh aryoonov chee luhvatsveer.

45 Give them face (fabric), they'll ask for the lining.
(No end to giving, greed.)

Երես տաս, աստառ կ'ուզէ։
Yeres das, astar goozen.

46 I don't want it, put it in my pocket.
(Being untruthfully polite.)

Չեմ ուզեր, ճէպս դիր։
Chem oozer, jebuhs (kuhrbanuhs) teer.

47 Luck and misfortune are brother and sister, they walk together.

Բախտ եւ անբախտ քոյր եղբայր են, իրարու հետ կը քալեն։
Pakhd yev anpakhd kooyr yekhpayr en, eeraroo hed guh kalen.

48 Don't love too much, there is hate; don't hate too much, there is love.
(There is a fine margin between love and hatred.)

Շատ մի՛ սիրեր, ատել կայ, շատ մի՛ ատեր, սիրել կայ։
Shad mee seerer, adel gah; shad mee ader, seerel gah.

49 He who falls in the well by himself will not cry.

Ինքնիրեն հորը ինկողը չի լար։
Eenkneeren horuh eengoghuh chee lar.

50 The lazy one's opportunity comes and settles on the knee.
(Luck.)

Ծոյլին բախտը կու գայ, ծունկին վրայ կը նստի։
Dzooyleen pakhduh goo kah, dzoongeen vrah guh nuhsdee.

51 Whatever you holler into the well echoes back to you.
(You reap what you sow.)

Հորին մէջ ինչ որ պոռաս, ան կ'իմանաս։
Horeen mech eench vor boras, an geemanas.

52 Be content with your condition; don’t look above yourself, look at those below yourself.
(Be grateful.)

Գոհ եղիր վիճակէդ, քեզմէ վերին մի, նայիր, քեզմէ վարին նայիր։
Koh yegheer veejaget, kezmeh vereen mee nayeer, kezmeh vareen nayeh.

53 When alive if you haven’t done, when dead you will never do.
(Do good when alive.)

Ողջ ըլլաս չես ըրած, մեռնիս նէ հէչ չես ըրած։
Voghch uhllas ches uhradz, mernees neh hech ches uhradz.

54 Elevate yourself, elevate others.

Բարձրացի՛ր, բարձրացո՛ւր։
Partsratseer, partsratsoor.

55 A righteous man may stagger, but he won’t fall.

Շիտակ մարդը սերսեմլեմիշ կ’ըլլայ, բայց վար չ’իյնար։
Sheedag martuh sersemlemeesh guhllah, payts var cheeynar.

56 Can’t make pilaf with her water.
(Can’t trust her.)

Անոր ջուրին փիլաւ չի ձգուիր։
Anor chooreen pilaf chee tsuhkveer.

57 A straight wall will never fall.

Շիտակ պատը չի փլիր։
Sheedag baduh chee puhleer.

58 We may sit crooked, but let’s talk straight.

Ծուռ նստինք՝ շիտակ խօսինք։
Dzoor nuhsdeenk, sheedag khoseenk.

59 When anything is cheap, the customer doesn’t have a conscience.
(Value is not recognized when cheap.)

Բան մը եթէ աժան է, յաճախորդը խիղճ չ’ունենար։
Pan muh yeteh azhan eh, hajakhortuh kheeghj choonenar.

60 Beware of jealousy, because jealousy will bite you first.

Զգուշացի՛ր նախանձէ, որովհետեւ նախ քեզ կը խածնէ։
Uhzkooshatseer nakhantseh, vorovhedev nakh kezee guh khadzneh.

61 Let me lie down, you can also eat me.
(Gluttony. Can be destroyed by gossip.)

Ես ալ պառկիմ, ինծի ալ կեր։
Yes al bargeem, eendzee al ger.

62 There is no such thing as complete happiness in this world.

Կատարեալ ուրախութիւն չի կայ այս աշխարհին մէջ:
Gadaryal oorakhootyoon chee gah ays ashkhareen mech.

63 If you carry him to Jerusalem, even then he will not be grateful.

Շալկած Երուսաղէմ տանիս, նորէն շնորհակալ չէ:
Shalgadz Yeroosaghem danees, noren shnorhagal cheh.

64 Wash the feet, drink the water. (Gratitude; thankfulness with humility.)

Ոտքը լուա՛, ջուրը խմէ:
Vodkuh luhvah, chooruh khuhmeh.

65 A crooked ruler cannot make a straight line.

Ծուռ քանակէն շիտակ գիծ չ'ելլեր:
Dzoor kanagen sheedag keedz cheller.

66 Don't think I came from a hole in the wall. (Respect me and my ancestors.)

Չխորհիս թէ պատին ծակէն ելայ:
Chuhkhorhees teh badeen dzagen yela.

67 Scratch the earth, may it turn to gold.

Հողը ճանկես, ոսկի դառնայ:
Hoghuh janges, vosgee tarnah.

68 If the world burns, I don't have a bundle of grass to hold on to. (Desperation.)

Աշխարհն այրի, խորոմ մը խոտ չունիմ:
Ashkharn ayree, khorom muh khod chooneem.

69 The knife doesn't chop its own handle. (Don't betray your loved one.)

Չախուն իր կոթը չի տաշեր:
Chakhoon eer gotuh chee dasher.

70 Nothing is as cheap as the most expensive.

Սուղէն աժանը չկայ:
Sooghen azhanuh chee gah.

71 If your ten fingers are lit like candles, they still will not see (understand).

Տասը մատդ մոմ ըլլայ եւ ամբողջ վառի, նորէն չեն տեսներ:
Dasuh maduht mom uhllah yev ampoghch varee, noren chen desner.

72 The empty barrel makes the most noise.

Պարապ տակառը շատ ձայն կը հանէ:
Barab dagaruh shad tsayn guh haneh.

73 Good apples placed next to rotten ones will spoil too.

Հոտած խնձորին քով լաւն ալ դնես, ան ալ կը հոտի:
Hodadz khuhntzoreen kov lavn al tuhnes, an al guh hodee.

74 When you see the Kurd, ask him for bread, so he won't ask you for bread. (Preempt him.)

Քիւրտը տեսնես հաց ուզէ, որ քիւրտը քեզմէ հաց չուզէ:
Kurduh desnes, hats oozeh, vor Kurduh kezmeh hats choozeh.

75 The fallen one has no friends.

Ինկողը բարեկամ չ'ունենար:
Eengoghuh paregam choonenar.

76 A sweet word can draw water from a rock.

Անուշ խօսքը քարէն ջուր կը հանէ:
Anoosh khoskuh karen choor guh haneh.

77 As much as you know, there's plenty more to learn.

Որքան բան գիտես, դեռ շատ սորվելիք ունիս:
Vorkan pan keedes, ter shad sorveleek oonees.

78 They take you to the water and bring you back thirsty. (Misled, unfulfilled.)

Ջուրը կը տանին՝ ծարաւ կը բերեն:
Chooruh guh daneen, dzarav guh peren.

79 As many languages as you know, that's how many persons you are.

Որքան լեզու գիտես այնքան մարդ ես:
Vorkan lezoo keedes aynkan mart es.

80 One is mud; one is tar. (One is worse than the other.)

Մէկը չամուր է, միւսը՝ կիֆթ:
Meguh chamoor eh, myoosuh zeeft.

81 Every single tongue (language) is worthy of being one man.

Ամէն մէկ լեզու մէկ մարդ կ'արժէ:
Amen meg lezoo meg mart garzheh.

82 My account (conscience) is clean.

Իմ հաշիւս մաքուր է:
Eem hasheevuhs makoor eh.

83 Spit in his face, he thinks the rain is coming. (Insensitive; no shame.)

Երեսը թքնես, կը խորհի անձրեւ կու գայ:
Yeresuh tuhknes, guh khorhee antsrev goo kah.

84 If you spit up, it's your ceiling; if you spit down, it's your beard.
(No-win situation.)

Վեր թքնես՝ տանիքդ է, վար թքնես մօրուքդ է:
Ver tuhknes, daneekuht eh, var tuhknes, morookuht eh.

85 The sound of the drum is pleasant from afar.
(Familiarity breeds contempt.)

Թմբուկի ձայնը հեռուէն հաճելի է:
Tuhmpoogee tsaynuh herooyen hajelee eh.

86 The sated one feeds the hungry one with small crumbs.

Կուշտը անօթիին մանր փշրեր է:
Gooshduh anoteeyeen manuhr puhshrer eh.

87 A tired man's work goes backward.

Յոգնած մարդուն գործը ետ կ'երթայ:
Hoknadz martoon kordzuh yed gertah.

88 Where there's a will, there's a (road) way.

Ուրտեղ կամք կայ, ճամբայ կայ:
Vordegh gamk gah, jampah gah.

89 The world is wide, my shoe is narrow, what's the use?
(Can't win; unlucky.)

Աշխարհը լայն է, կօշիկս նեղ է, օգուտը ի՞նչ է:
Ashkharuh layn eh, gosheeguhs negh eh, okooduh eench eh?

90 Cursing is likened to an apronful of stones; if one doesn't strike, another one will.

Անէծքը գոգնոց մը լեցուն քար է, մէկը չդպնայ միւսը կը դպնայ:
Anedzkuh koknots muh letsoon kar eh, meguh chutuhbnah, myoosuh guh tuhbnah.

91 Find the new, then throw away the old.

Նորը գտիր, ետքէն հինը նետէ:
Noruh kuhdeer, yedken heenuh nedeh.

92 The curse comes full circle.

Անէծքը անիծողին կը դառնայ:
Anedzkuh aneedzogheen guh tarnah.

93 Where there is bread, there is no mouth (hunger); where there is mouth (hunger), there is no bread.
(Needs not fulfilled.)

Ուր հաց կայ, բերան չի կայ, ուր բերան կայ, հաց չի կայ:
Oor hats gah, peran chee gah; oor peran gah, hats chee gah.

94 With the dry cloth the wet also burns.
(Sometimes evil overcomes goodness.)

Չոր կտաւին հետ թացն ալ կ'այրի:
Chor guhdaveen hed tatsn al gayree.

95 Lie is obtuse.
(Not effective.)

Սուտը բութ է:
Sooduh poot eh.

96 The prophet has no respect in his hometown.

Մարգարէն իր քաղաքին մէջ յարգ չունի:
Markaren eer kaghakeen mech hark choonee.

97 Coarse or fine, thick or thin, is one price. Woe to the fine spinner.
(Use time wisely.)

Հաստ ու բարակ մէկ գին է, վա՛յ բարակ մանողին:
Hasd oo parag meg keen, vay parag manogheern.

98 Worn out, burned out person.
(He's a scoundrel; wild person.)

Հանած վարած մէկն է:
Hanadz varadz megn eh.

99 He's worn out his mother's homespun.
(Wasteful.)

Մօրը մանածը մաշեցուցած է:
Moruh manadzuh mashetsootsadz eh.

100 Before seeing the water, she gathers her skirt.
(Foresight.)

Ջուրը չտեսած փէշերը կը սօթտէ:
Chooruh chuhdesadz pesheruh guh sotteh.

101 Let evil take it away.

Չարը տանի:
Charuh danee.

102 Good you came, a thousand greetings.
(We are so glad to see you.)

Բարի եկաք, հազար բարի:
Paree yegak, hazar paree.

103 Looks for hairs in the eggs.
(Fussy, persnickety.)

Հաւկիթին մէջ մազ կը փնտռէ:
Havgeeteen mech maz guh puhndreh.

104 He sat on the ashes.
(Financially wiped out.)

Մոխիրին վրայ նստաւ:
Mokheereen vrah nuhsdav.

105 Pulled the days with a rope.
(Tough life.)

Օրերը չուանով քաշեցի:
Oreruh chuhvanov kashetzee.

106 They judge man from the eye of the needle.
(Extreme fault-finding.)

Ասեղին ծակէն մարդ կը դիտեն:
Asegheen dzagen mart guh teeden.

107 Fed with a spoon, removed the eye with the handle.
(Goodness obliterated by evildoing.)

Դգալով կերցուց, կոթով աչքը հանեց:
Tuhkalov gertsoots, gotov achkuh hanets.

108 You can hear from the stone, but you can't hear from him.
(Aloofness; no communication.)

Քարէն ձայն կայ, իրմէ ձայն չի կայ:
Karen tsayn gah, eermeh tsayn chee gah.

109 If speech is known to be silver, yet silence is golden.

Եթէ խօսքը արծաթ է, լռութիւնը ոսկի է սակայն:
Yeteh khoskuh ardzat eh, luhrootyoonuh vosgee eh, sagayn.

110 The world's treasures remain with the world.

Աշխարհին գանձը աշխարհին կը մնայ:
Ashkhareen kantsuh askhareen guh muhnah.

111 From mouth to mouth, the mote becomes a log.
(Gossip, exaggeration.)

Բերնէ բերան՝ կ'ըլլայ գերան:
Perneh peran guhllah keran.

112 The deprived one lives; woe to the depriver.

Զրկուողը ապրեր է, վա՜յ զրկողին:
Zuhrguhvoghuh abrer eh, vay zuhrgogheen.

113 Burned his mouth on hot milk, so he blows on the yogurt.
(Hesitant, taking precautionary measures.)

Կաթէն բերանը այրեցաւ, մածունին վրայ կը փչէ:
Gatehn peranuh ayretsav, madzooneen vrah guh puhcheh.

114 The empty wheat stalk raises its head.
(No substance.)

Պարապ ցորենի հասկը գլուխը կը բարձրացնէ:
Barab tsorenee hasguh kuhlookhuh guh partsratsuhneh.

115 Don't eat (abuse) the rights of others.

Ուրիշին իրաւունքը մի՛ ուտեր:
Ooreesheen eeravoonkuh mee ooder.

116 I haven't eaten onion, so my stomach can't hurt.
(There is no fear with prevention.)

Սոխ չեմ կերած որ փորս ցաւի:
Sokh chem gerads vor poruhs tsavee.

117 A friend to all is a friend to none.

Ամէնուն բարեկամը ոչ մէկուն բարեկամը չէ:
Amenoon paregamuh voch megoon paregamuh cheh.

118 Never the thorn will be a fig, nor the raspberry a grape.
(Whatever is, is.)

Ո՛չ տատասկը թուզ կը դառնայ, ոչ ալ մորենին՝ խաղող:
Voch dadasguh tooz guh tarnah, voch al moreneen khaghogh.

119 He who does not hear (understand) with his ear will hear (understand) with his back (stick).

Ան որ չի լսեր ականջով, կը լսէ կռնակով:
Ahn vor chee luhser aganchov, guh luhseh guhrnagov.

120 Keep your door closed, so you won't catch your neighbor at thievery.

Դուռդ գոց պահէ, դրացիդ գող մի՛ բռներ:
Tooruht kots baheh, tuhratseet kogh mee puhrner.

121 Who stands up in anger sits with harm.
(The quick-tempered will come to harm.)

Բարկութեամբ ոտքի ելլողը՝ վնասով կը նստի:
Pargootyamp vodkee yelloghuh vuhnasov guh nuhsdee.

122 Don't judge, so you won't be judged.

Մի՛ դատեր որ չդատուիս:
Mee tader, vor chuhtadvees.

123 A tree stands taller when it knows its roots.

Ծառը աւելի հպարտ կը կենայ, եթէ գիտնայ իր արմատները:
Dzaruh avelee huhbard guh genah, yeteh keedeh eer armadneruh.

124 If you like the rose, you must also like the thorn.

Վարդը սիրես, փուշն ալ պիտի սիրես:
Vartuh seeres, pooshn al beedee seeres.

125 Every rose has its thorn.

Ամէն վարդ իր փուշն ունի:
Amen vart eer pooshn oonee.

126 If a tree sways with every wind, it will lose all its leaves.
(Steadfast. Hold firm to convictions.)

Եթէ ամէն հովին երերայ, ծառին վրայ տերեւ չի մնար:
Yeteh amen hoveen jererah, dzareen vuhrah derev chee muhnar.

127 A tree sways with its leaves.
(Contentment within.)

Ծառը իր տերեւով կ'երերայ:
Dzaruh eer derevov gererah.

128 On every tree grows good and bad fruit.

Ամէն ծառին վրայ լաւ պտուղ ալ կը բուսնի, գէշ ալ:
Amen dzareen vrah lav buhdoogh al guh poosnee, kesh al.

129 The leaves don't rustle unless the wind is blowing.
(Cause and effect.)

Տերեւը չի խշրտար մինչեւ հովը փչէ:
Derevuh chee khuhshuhrdar meenchev hovuh puhcheh.

130 The flooded mill will not turn.
(Much is not always effective.)

Լեցուած ջուրով ջաղացքը չի դառնար:
Letsvadz choorov chaghatskuh chee tarnar.

131 Stones are not cast at a fruitless tree.

Անպտուղ ծառին քար չեն նետեր:
Anbuhdoogh dzareen kar chen neder.

132 The tree is recognized by its fruit.

Ծառը իր պտուղէն կը ճանչցուի:
Dzaruh eer buhdooghen guh janchtsuhvee.

133 When I have honey, flies come even from Baghdad.
(Money talks.)

Երբ մեղր ունիմ՝ ճանճերը Պաղտատէն ալ կու գան:
Yerp meghuhr ooneem janjeruh Baghdaden al goo kan.

134 The flowers fall under the bush.
(Goodness is not recognized.)

Ծաղիկը մացառին տակ կ'իյնայ:
Dzagheeguh matsareen daguh geeyna.

135 There are many stones thrown at the fruit tree.

Պտղատու ծառին շատ քար նետող կ'ըլլայ:
Buhdghadoo dzareen shad kar nedogh guhllah.

136 The mature, crooked tree cannot be straightened.

Ծուռ մեծցած ծառը չի շտկուիր:
Dzoor medztsadz dzaruh chee shuhdguhveer.

137 Where the fire falls, there it burns.

Կրակը ինկած տեղը կ'այրէ:
Guhraguh eengadz deghuh gayreh.

138 The green leaf burns with the dry. (The good is destroyed with the bad.)

Կանաչ տերեւը չորին հետ կ'այրի:
Ganach derevuh choreen hed gayree.

139 Wish well for your neighbor, so goodness will come to your head.

Բարի ուզէ դրացիիդ որ բարի գայ գլխուդ:
Paree oozeh tuhratseeyeet, vor paree kah kuhlkhoot.

140 The thief who steals eggs will also steal chickens.

Հավկիթին գողը հաւ ալ կը գողնայ:
Havgeeteen koghuh hav al guh koghnah.

141 Eat with your friend, but do not do business with him.

Բարեկամիդ հետ հաց կեր, բայց առեւտուր մի՛ ըներ:
Paregameet hed hats ger, payts arevdoor mee uhner.

142 Until you eat a kilo of salt with your friend, you won't know who he is. (Many experiences test a friend.)

Մինչեւ որ քիլօ մը աղ չուտես բարեկամիդ հետ, չես գիտեր թէ ով է:
Meenchev vor kilo muh agh choodes paregameet hed, ches keeder teh ov eh.

143 Have intelligent enemies, but don't have foolish friends.

Խելացի թշնամի ունեցիր, բայց խենթ բարեկամ մի՛ ունենար:
Khelatsee tuhshnamee oonetseer, payts khent paregam mee oonenar.

144 It is more acceptable to have an intelligent enemy than to have an ignorant friend.

Աւելի նախընտրելի է խելացի թշնամի ունենալ, քան թէ տգէտ բարեկամ:
Avelee nakhuhndrelee eh khelatsee tuhshnamee oonenal, kan teh duhked paregam.

145 Tell me who your friend is, and I'll tell you who you are.

Ըսէ ինծի բարեկամդ ով է, ըսեմ քեզի թէ դուն ով ես:
Uhseh eendzee paregamuht ov eh, uhsem kezee teh toon ov es.

146 All who laugh in your face are not your friends.

Ամէն երեսիդ խնդացողը բարեկամդ չէ:
Amen yereseet khuhntatsoghuh paregamuht cheh.

147 A known enemy cannot be a friend to the Armenian.

Գիտցած թշնամին հայուն բարեկամ չ'ըլլար:
Keedtsadz tshnameen hayoon paregam chuhllar.

148 There is no giver of bread to the orphan, but many givers of advice.

Որբին հաց տուող չ'ըլլար, բայց խրատ տուող շատ կ'ըլլայ:
Vorpeen hats duhvogh chuhllar, payts khuhrad duhvogh shad.

149 Don't be afraid of the obvious enemy, be afraid of the secret one.

Յայտնի թշնամիէն մի՛ վախնար, գաղտնի թշնամիէն վախցիր:
Haydnee tuhshameeyen mee vakhnar, kaghdnee tuhshnameeyen vakhtseer.

150 The old enemy can't be a friend.

Հին թշնամին բարեկամ չ'ըլլար:
Heen tushnameen paregam chuhllar.

151 The more you call a man a fool, the more foolish he becomes.

Մարդուն որչափ յիմար ըսես, կը յիմարանայ:
Martoon vorchap heemar uhses, guh heemaranah.

152 The traveler's heaviest burden is an empty wallet.

Ճամբորդին ամենածանր բեռը պարապ քսակն է:
Jamporteen amenadzanuhr peruh barab kuhsagn eh.

153 One shame for the beggar, a double shame for the nongiver.
(A double shame for the uncharitable.)

Ուզողին՝ մէկ ամօթ, չտուողին՝ երկու ամօթ:
Oozogheen meg amot, chuhduhvogheen yergoo amot.

154 Go die, come (back), then I will love you.
(Unappreciated while alive.)

Գնա՛ մեռիր, եկուր սիրեմ:
Kuhnah mereer, yegoor seerem.

155 Hope is the bread of the unfortunate.

Յոյսը դժբախտներուն հացն է:
Hooysuh tuhzhpakhdneroon hatsn eh.

156 The fool is never unlucky, the wise man is never happy.

Ապուշը բնաւ դժբախտ չէ, խելօքը միշտ ուրախ չէ:
Abooshuh puhnav tuhzhpakhd cheh, khelokuh meeshd oorakh cheh.

157 The poor longs for bread, the rich for everything.

Աղքատը կարօտ է հացի, հարուստը ամէն բանի:
Aghkaduh garod eh hatsee, haroosduh amen panee.

158 False words, false money come from a false person.

Սուտ խօսքը, սուտ դրամը, սուտ մարդէն կու գայ:
Sood khoskuh, sood tuhramuh, sood marten goo kah.

159 Fire broke out at the liar's house, but nobody believed him.

Սուտ խօսողին տունը կրակ ինկաւ, ոչ ոք հաւատաց:
Sood khosogheen doonuh guhrag eengav, voch vok havadatz.

160 When a poor man extends his hand, it is not for a greeting.

Երբ աղքատը ձեռքը կ'երկնցնէ, բարեւելու համար չէ:
Yerp aghkad muh tserkuh gerguhntsuhneh, pareveloo hamar cheh.

161 A lie destroys the liar's home.

Սուտը սուտ ասողին տունն է քանդում:
Sooduh sood asogheen doonn eh kantoom.

162 Laughter is abundant in the mouths of fools.

Խնդուքը առատ է ապուշներու բերնին մէջ:
Khuhntookuh arad eh abooshneroon perneen mech.

163 When the peasant is poor, the country is poor.

Երբ աղքատ է գիւղացին՝ աղքատ է երկիրը:
Yerp aghkad eh kyooghatseen, aghkad eh yergeeruh.

164 A man's personality doesn't change until his soul leaves him.	Մինչեւ մարդուն հոգին դուրս չելլէ, բնութիւնը դուրս չ'ելլեր: *Meenchev martoon hokeen toors chelleh, puhnootyoonuh toors cheller.*
165 The tailor's pocket has a hole in it.	Դերձակին գրպանը ծակ կ'ըլլայ: *Tertsageen kuhrbanuh dzag guhllah.*
166 Every woman makes her own style of yogurt.	Ամէն կին իր գիտցած մածունը կը շինէ: *Amen geen eer keedtsadz madzoonuh guh sheeneh.*
167 Gossip is said behind the king's back.	Թագաւորին ետեւէն խօսք կ'ըսեն: *Takavoreen yedeven khosk guhsen.*
168 The fool's yarn is spun by the wind. (The fool's word has no worth.)	Խենթին մանածը հովը կը մանէ: *Khenteen mahnadzuh hovuh guh maneh.*
169 Man with man. (Survival means interaction.)	Մարդը մարդով է: *Martuh martov eh.*
170 Look for your enemy under your pillow. (The enemy can come from within.)	Թշնամիդ բարձին տակը փնտռէ: *Tuhshnameet partseet daguh puhndreh.*
171 He grew, pain grew. (Problems grow with the child.)	Մեծցաւ, մեծ ցաւ: *Medztsav, medz tsav.*
172 He doesn't have face. (No shame.)	Երես չունի: *Yeres choonee.*
173 A crooked man always speaks crooked.	Սխալ մարդը միշտ սխալ կը խօսի: *Skhal martuh meeshd skhal guh khossi.*
174 Who is running after you? (What's the hurry?)	Ետեւէդ վազողը ո՞վ է: *Yedevet vazoghuh ohv eh?*
175 The dish breaks, the crack remains. (Wrong words never heal.)	Ամանը կը կոտրի, ճեղքը կը մնայ: *Amanuh guh godree, jeghkuh guh mna.*

176 When they are giving money, they are shaking.
(They are stingy.)

Փարայ պիտի տան՝ կը դողան:
Para beedee dahn, guh toghahn.

177 Do good, and you don’t know in what form it will come back.
(Do good, and it will return to you one way or another.)

Բարիք ըրէ, չես գիտեր ինչ ձեւով ետ կու գայ:
Pareek ereh, chehs keeder eench tsevov yed gooka.

178 The bread and the water are lacking.
(Needy, never satisfied.)

Հացը ջուրը պակաս է:
Hatsuh, chooruh bagahs eh.

179 The dog’s kaka doesn’t remain under the snow.
(Truth will always be exposed.)

Շունին քաքը ձիւնին տակը չի մնար:
Shooneen kakuh tsyuneen dahguh chee menar.

180 Talk about a good man, and he appears (out of nowhere).

Լաւ մարդը իր խօսքին վրայ կու գայ:
Lahv mahrtuh eer khoskeen vrah gooka.

181 I will deal you justice.
(I will get even with you.)

Հաղդ կու գամ:
Haghuht goo kam.

182 His word comes to nothing.
(Not trustworthy.)

Խօսքը բանի տեղ չի գար:
Khoskuh panee degh chee kar.

183 His face is torn.
(Shameless.)

Երեսը պատռած է:
Yeressuh bahdradz eh.

184 Whatever you do now, that is what will remain.
(Good deeds don’t die.)

Ինչ որ ընես՝ ատի կը մնայ:
Eench vohr enehss, ahdee guh menah.

185 The one who speaks the truth has a hole in the head.
(Being truthful brings scorn.)

Շիտակ խօսողին թէփէն ծակ կ’ըլլայ:
Sheedahg khossogheen tehpehn dzahg guhllah.

186 Don’t carry the ladder horizontally.
(Don’t complicate things.)

Սանդուխը լայնքին մի՛ շալկեր:
Santookhuh laynkeen mee shahlguehr.

Եթէ ամէն հովին երերայ, ծառին վրայ տերեւ չի մնար։

8

Nature

"If a tree sways with every wind, it will lose all its leaves."

1 Escaped the rain, got caught in the hail. (Bad to worse.)

Անձրեւէն փախանք, կարկուտին բռնուեցանք:
Antsreven pakhank, gargoodeen puhrnuhvetsank.

2 The sea won't rest until it becomes stormy.

Ծովը մինչեւ չալեկոծի, չի հանդարտիր:
Dzovuh meenchev chalegodzee, chee hantardeer.

3 The mountain can't come to the mountain, but man can come to man. (Being helpful.)

Լեռը լերան չի հանդիպիր, մարդը մարդուն կը հանդիպի:
Leruh leran chee hanteebeer, martuh martoon guh hanteebee.

4 Spring doesn't come with one flower.

Մէկ ծաղիկով գարուն չի գար:
Meg dzaghigov karoon chee kar.

5 Planted, reaped the pea; because you went to the market, did you become a chick pea?
(Pretention.)

Ցանած, քաղած սիսեռը, շուկայ գացիր լէպլէպի՞ եղար:
Tsanadz, kaghadz seeseruh, shoogah katseer leblebee yeghar?

6 Whatever you plant, that's what you will reap.

Ինչ որ ցանես, այն կը հնձես:
Eench vor tsanes, ayn guh huhntses.

7 Large mountain, large cloud.
(Much demands much.)

Մեծ լեռ, մեծ ամպ:
Medz ler, medz amb.

8 A tree stands taller when it knows its roots.

Ծառը աւելի հպարտ կը կենայ, եթէ գիտէ իր արմատները:
Dzaruh avelee huhbard guh genah, yeteh keedeh eer armadneruh.

9 If you like the rose, you must also like the thorn.

Վարդը սիրես, փուշն ալ պիտի սիրես:
Vartuh seeres, pooshn al beedee seeres.

10 Every rose has its thorn.

Ամէն վարդ իր փուշն ունի:
Amen vart eer pooshn oonee.

11 If a tree sways with every wind, it will lose all its leaves.
(Steadfast.)

Եթէ ամէն հովին երերայ, ծառին վրայ տերեւ չի մնար:
Yeteh amen hoveen yererah, dzareen vrah derev chee muhnar.

12 A tree sways with its leaves.
(Contentment within.)

Ծառը իր տերեւով կ'երերայ:
Dzaruh eer derevov gererah.

13 You will find good and bad fruit on one tree.

Մէկ ծառին վրայ լաւ պտուղ ալ կը բուսնի, գէշ ալ:
Meg dzareen vuhrah lav buhdoogh al guh poosnee, kesh al.

14 The trash should be planted in the garden.
(Make use of everything; bury the bad; be frugal.)

Աղբը պարտէզը պիտի ցանես:
Aghpuh bardezuh beedee tsanes.

15 Crossed the sea, drowned in the brook.
(Did the impossible, was overtaken by the possible.)

Ծովը անցաւ, առուին մէջ խեղդուեցաւ:
Dzovuh antsav, arooyeen mech kheghtuhvetsav.

16 The leaves don't rustle unless the wind is blowing.
(Cause and effect.)

Տերեւը չի խշրտար մինչեւ հովը փչէ:
Derevuh chee khuhshuhrdar meenchev hovuh puhcheh.

17 The flooded mill will not turn.
(Much is not always effective.)

Լեցուած ջուրով ջաղացքը չի դառնար:
Letsvadz choorov chaghatskuh chee tarnar.

18 He who falls in the sea will reach for the foam.
(Desperation.)

Ծովն ինկողը ձեռքը փրփուրին կը նետէ:
Dzovn eengoghuh tserkuh puhrpooreen guh nedeh.

19 Stones are not cast at a fruitless tree.

Անպտուղ ծառին քար չեն նետեր:
Anbuhdoogh dzareen kar chen neder.

20 The tree is recognized by its fruit.

Ծառը իր պտուղէն կը ճանչցուի:
Dzaruh eer buhdooghen guh janchtsuhvee.

21 When I have honey, flies come even from Baghdad.
(Money talks.)

Երբ մեղր ունիմ, ճանճերը Պաղտատէն ալ կու գան:
Yerp meghur ooneem, janjeruh Baghdaden al goo kan.

22 The flowers fall under the bush.
(Goodness is not recognized.)

Ծաղիկը մացառին տակը կ'իյնայ:
Dzagheeguh matsareen daguh geeynah.

23 Let the wind blow, let the water flood the world, I don't care.

Հովը թող փչէ, ջուրը թող ջրէ աշխարհը, հոգս չէ:
Hovuh togh pucheh, chooruh togh chuhreh ashkharuh, hokuhs cheh.

24 Every tree has its own shade.
(Every person is a worthy individual.)

Ամէն ծառ իր շուքը ունի:
Amen dzar eer shookuh oonee.

25 There are many stones thrown at the fruit trees.

Պտղատու ծառին շատ քար նետող կ'ըլլայ:
Buhdghadoo dzareen shad kar nedogh guhllah.

26 The mature, crooked tree cannot be straightened.

Ծուռ մեծցած ծառը չի շտկուիր:
Dzoor medztsadz dzaruh chee shuhdguhveer.

27 Where the fire falls, there it burns.

Կրակը ինկած տեղը կ'այրէ:
Guhraguh eengadz deghuh gayreh.

28 The empty wheat stalk raises its head.
(No substance.)

Պարապ ցորենի հասկը գլուխը կը բարձրացնէ:
Barab tsorenee hasguh kuhlookhuh guh partsratsuhneh.

29 The green leaf burns with the dry.
(The good is destroyed with the bad.)

Կանաչ տերեւը չորին հետ կ'այրի:
Ganach derevuh choreen hed gayree.

30 Armenians can squeeze water from the stone.
(Armenians are resourceful and frugal.)

Հայերը քարէն ջուր կը հանեն:
Hayeruh karen choor guh hanen.

Nature

31 If the mountain does not suit you, you must adapt to the mountain.

Լեռը քեզի չի յարմարիր, դուն լերան պիտի յարմարիս։
Leruh kezee chee harmareer, toon leran beedee harmarees.

32 Don't step into the water unless you can see the bottom.

Ան ջուրը որուն տակը չես տեսներ, մէջը մի՛ մտներ։
An chooruh voroon daguh ches desner, mechuh mee muhdnar.

33 Even the water and the silt from the stream are helpful to the ocean.

Գետին ջուրն ու տիղմն ալ ծովին օգուտ ունին։
Kedeen choorn oo deeghmn al dzoveen okood ooneen.

34 What you learn in childhood is carved into stone; what you learn in old age is carved into ice.

Պզտիկութեանդ սորվածը քարին վրայ կը փորագրուի, մեծահասակ ժամանակ սորվածդ՝ սառոյցի։
Buhzdeegootyanuht sorvadzuh kareen vrah guh porakuhrvee; medzahasag zhamanag sorvadzuht sarooytsee.

35 Until you see the water, don't remove your shoes.

Ջուրը չտեսած՝ կօշիկդ մի՛ հաներ։
Chooruh chuhdesadz gosheeguht mee haner.

36 A rolling stone holds no moss.
(No roots.)

Գլորուող քարը մամուռ չի բռներ։
Kuhlorvogh karuh mamoor chee puhrner.

37 Do good, cast in the water; it will return and find you.

Բարիք ըրէ ջուրը նետէ, անիկա կու գայ քեզի կը գտնէ։
Pareek uhreh chooruh nedeh; aneegah goo kah kezee guh kuhdneh.

38 He builds castles in the air.
(He is delusional.)

Օդին մէջ դղեակներ կը շինէ։
Oteen mech tughyagner guh sheeneh.

39 Puts water in the mortar and beats it.
(Inappropriate use; fighting a losing battle.)

Ջուրը հրասանդին մէջ դրած կը ծեծէ։
Chooruh huhrsanteen mech tuhradz guh dzedzeh.

40 Don't drop your sugar in the water.
(Don't waste.)

Շաքարդ ջուրը մի՛ ձգեր:
Shakaruht chooruh mee tsuhker.

41 There isn't anything harder than soil.
(Problems need to be worked out to produce results.)

Հողէն դժուարը չկայ:
Hoghen tuhzhvaruh chee gah.

42 Doesn't see the beam in his eye, sees the sliver in the eyes of others.

Իր աչքին գերանը չի տեսներ, ուրիշին աչքին շիւղը կը տեսնէ:
Eer achkeen keranuh chee desner, ooreesheen achkeen shyooghuh guh desneh.

43 Only a handful of soil can satiate the eye of man.
(It's enough, but man wants more.)

Մարդոց աչքը միայն ափ մը հողով կը կշտանայ:
Martots achkuh meeayn ahp muh hoghov guh guhshdanah.

44 Fire fell on the heart.
(Heartbreak and sudden disaster.)

Կրակ մը ինկաւ սրտին վրայ:
Guhrag muh eengav seerdeen vrah.

45 Even if your jaw were to fall into the water, it wouldn't stop.
(You talk too much.)

Ջենկեդ ջուրն ալ իյնայ չի կայնիր:
Chenget choorn al eeynah, chee gayneer.

46 There are two things you can't stare at with your eyes: the sun and death.

Երկու բան կայ որ կարելի չէ աչքերը սեւեռած դիտել, արեւը եւ մահը:
Yergoo pan gah vor garelee cheh achkeruh severadz teedel- arevuh yev mahuh.

47 My blood turned to water.
(I was frightened.)

Արիւնս ջուր կտրեցաւ:
Aryoonuhs choor guhdretzav.

48 The father is the flood, the mother is the dam.
(The father is the spender, the mother is the conserver.)

Հայրը սել է, մայրը պէնտ է:
Hayruh sel eh, mayruh bend eh.

49 Your child is like a flower, to look upon and be joyful.

Զաւակը ծաղիկ մըն է, վրան կը նայիս կ'ուրախանաս:
Zavaguh dzagheeg muhn eh, vrahn guh nayees goorakhanas.

50 The shade of the son-in-law, the shade of the thorn.
(No benefit from either one.)

Փեսային շուքն է, փուշին շուքն է:
Pesayeen shookn eh, poosheen shookn eh.

51 Man's worst enemies are a bad wife and cold weather.
(Both are intolerable.)

Մարդուն ամենէն մեծ թշնամիներն են գէշ կինը եւ ցուրտ օդը:
Martoon amenen medz tuhshnameenern en kesh geenuh yev tsoord otuh.

52 Pure oil doesn't stay under the water.
(Goodness always surfaces.)

Արդար իւղը ջուրին տակ չի մնար:
Artar yooghuh chooreen dag chee muhnar.

53 It was asked of the fish, "What news do you have from the sea?" The fish said, "I have much to say, but my mouth is full of water."
(Ask the person who knows.)

Ձուկին հարցուցին, «Ծովէն ի՞նչ լուր», ըսաւ «Շատ բան ունիմ ըսելիք, բայց բերանս ջուրով լեցուն է»:
Tsoogeen hartsootseen, "Dzoven eench loor?" Uhsav, "Shad pan ooneem uhseleek, payts peranuhs choorov letsoon eh."

54 Do good, and throw it into the sea. If the one that receives doesn't appreciate it, the fish will.
(Someone benefits.)

Բարիք մը ըրէ, ծովը նետէ- եթէ առնողը չի գիտնար, ձուկը կը գիտնայ:
Pareek muh uhreh, dzovuh nedeh. Yeteh arnoghuh chee keednah, tsooguh guh keednah.

55 Throw your bread into the sea. If the wave doesn't notice, the fish will.
(Someone benefits.)

Հացդ ծովը նետէ, ալիքը չի գիտնայ, ձուկը կը գիտնայ:
Hatsuht dzovuh nedeh, aleekuh chee keednah, tsooguh guh keednah.

56 The dog's kaka doesn't remain under the snow.
(Truth will always be exposed.)

Շունին քաքը ձիւնին տակ չի մնար:
Shooneen kakuh tsyooneen daguh chee muhnar.

57 Don't hope for whiteness; snow is white, too, but the dogs dirty it.

Ճերմակութեան մի փափաքիր, ձիւնն ալ ճերմակ է, շուները վրան կ'աղտոտեն:
Jermagootyan mee papakeer; tsyoonn al jermag eh, shooneruh vuhran gaghdoden.

58 The hen, which is a hen, when drinking water looks up (to heaven). (Gratitude.)	Հաւը որ հաւ է, ջուր խմէ նէ, վեր կը նայի։ *Havuh vor hav eh, choor khuhmeh neh, ver guh nayee.*
59 When drinking water, the crow looks upward (to heaven). (Gratitude.)	Ղուշը ջուր խմէ նէ, երվան կը նայի։ *Ghooshuh choor khuhmeh neh, yervan guh nayee.*
60 The butterfly went up the tree, what is and what isn't (everything) dropped down. (Impossible situation.)	Թիթեռնիկը ծառ է ելեր, ինչ կայ չի կայ վար է թափեր։ *Teeterneeguh dzar eh yeler, eench gah chee gah var eh taper.*
61 The fly isn't dirty, but when it falls in the water, it spoils the appetite.	Ճանճը փիս չէ, բայց ջուրին մէջ իյնայ ախորժակ կ՚աւրէ։ *Janjuh pees cheh, payts chooreen mech eeynah akhorzhag gavreh.*
62 "Father, what thing flies the fastest, the moon, the stars, the sun, or the birds?" The father thinks and answers, "Son, time flies ahead the fastest."	«Հայրիկ, ի՞նչ բանն ամենէն արագը կը թռի – լուսի՞նը, աստղե՞րը, արե՞ւը կամ թռչունները»։ Հայրը կը խորհի ու կը պատասխանէ.- «Տղաս, ժամանակը կ՚անցնի ամենէն առաջ»։ *"Hayreeg, eench pan amenen arakuh guh tuhree, looseenuh, asdgheruh, arevuh gam tuhrchoonneruh?" Hayruh guh khorhee oo guh badashkhaneh, "Duhghas, zhamanaguh gantsnee amenen arach."*
63 The orphan poured water on his head, heaven and earth darkened. (Unfortunate.)	Որբը գլուխը ջուր դրեր է, երկինք եւ գետին մթներ են։ *Vorpuh kuhlookhuh choor turer eh, yergeenk yev kedeen muhtner en.*
64 It is very sweet, but underneath is a thorn.	Շատ անուշ է, բայց տակը փուշ է։ *Shad anoosh eh, payts daguh poosh eh.*
65 Whatever I say, write it on ice. (What I say is meaningless.)	Ինչ որ ըսեմ, սառին վրայ գրէ։ *Eench vor uhsem, sareen vrah kuhreh.*

66 Can't make pilaf with her water.
(Can't trust her.)

Անոր ջուրին փիլաւ չի ձգուիր:
Anor chooreen peelav chee tsuhkveer.

67 Scratch the earth, may it turn to gold.

Հողը ճանկես, ոսկի դառնայ:
Hoghuh janges, vosgee tarnah.

68 One is mud; the other is tar.
(Mud can be washed; tar cannot. One is worse than the other.)

Մէկը չամուր է, միւսը՝ զիֆթ:
Meguh chamoor eh, myoosuh zift.

69 Spit in his face, he thinks the rain is coming.
(Insensitive.)

Երեսը թքնես, կը խորհի անձրեւ կու գայ:
Yeresuh tuhknes, guh khorhee antsrev goo kah.

70 Before seeing the water, she gathers her skirt.

Ջուրը չտեսած փէշերը կը սօթտէ:
Chooruh chuhdesadz pesheruh guh sotteh.

71 Never the thorn will be a fig, nor the raspberry a grape.
(Whatever is, is.)

Ո՛չ տատասկը թուզ կը դառնայ, ո՛չ ալ մորենին՝ խաղող:
Voch dadasguh tooz guh tarnah, voch al moreneen khaghogh.

72 The fool dropped a rock in the well; ten wise men couldn't pull it up.

Խենթը քար մը ձգեց հորը, տասը խելօք չկրցան հանել այն:
Khentuh kar muh tsuhkets horuh, dasuh khelok chuhguhrtzan hanel ayn.

73 The thief awaits a cloudy day.

Գողը ամպոտ օրուայ կը սպասէ:
Koghuh ambod orvah guh sbaseh.

74 Our real grave is not in the ground but in the hearts of people.

Մեր իրական գերեզմանը հողին մէջ չէ, այլ մարդոց սրտին մէջ:
Mer eeragan kerezmanuh hogheen mech cheh, ayl martots seerdeen mech.

75 An uninvited guest sits on thorns.
(Uncomfortable, uneasy.)

Անհրաւէր հիւրը փուշի վրայ կը նստի:
Anheraver hyooruh pooshee vrah guh nuhsdee.

76 The fool's yarn is spun by the wind.

Խենթին մանածը հովը կը մանէ:
Khenteen manadzuh hovuh guh maneh.

77 The poor man went to steal, the moon came out.
(No luck.)

Աղքատը գողութեան ելաւ, լուսին ծագեցաւ:
Aghkahduh koghootyan yelav, looseen dzaketzav.

78 May I die to your sun.
(I adore you.)

Արեւիդ մեռնիմ:
Areveet merneem.

79 Once the nightingale leaves the cage, he will not return.
(Lost opportunity.)

Պուլպուլը եթէ վանդակէն փախի ետ չի վերադառնար:
Boolbooluh yeteh vantaguen pakhee, yed chee veratarnar.

80 I am a ripe pear.
(My days are over.)

Հասած տանձ մըն եմ:
Hassadz dants men em.

81 The bread and the water are lacking.
(Needy, never satisfied.)

Հացը ջուրը պակաս է:
Hatsuh, chooruh bagahs eh.

82 May the soil be light on the grave.
(Rest in peace.)

Հողը թեթեւ ըլլայ գերեզմանին վրայ:
Hoghuh tetev ella kerezmaneen vrah.

83 The green leaves burn with the dry leaves.
(The good is destroyed with the bad.)

Կանանչ տերեւը չորին հետ կ'այրի:
Ganach derevuh chohreen hed gayree.

84 Armenians can squeeze water from the stone.
(Armenians are resourceful and frugal.)

Հայը քարէն ջուր կը հանէ:
Hayuh kahren choor guh haneh.

85 The smoke dissipated.
(He is tired and fed up.)

Մուխը մարաւ:
Mookhuh marav.

86 Let the owner enjoy the land.
(Let the owner enjoy the fruit of his labor.)

Հողը տէրը թող վայելէ:
Hoghuh dehruh togh vayeleh.

87 I will bring water for you with a sieve.
(I will work tirelessly for you; will do the impossible.)

Քեզի համար մաղով ջուր պիտի բերեմ:
Kezee hamar maghov choor beedee pehrehm.

88 The water went and found the road. (Returning to your roots. Truth will prevail.)

Ջուրը գնաց ճամբան գտաւ:
Chooruh kenats jahmpahn kdahv.

89 He fights with his kaka. (Everything is a problem for him.)

Քաքին հետ կը կռուի:
Kahkeen hed guh guervee.

90 Pear head. (Stupid.)

Տանձի գլուխ:
Dantsee kelookh.

91 Every man has a pain, every tree has a worm.

Ամէն մարդ ցաւ ունի, ամէն ծառ որդ ունի:
Amen mart tsav oonee, amen dzar vort oonee.

Հարսը Պաղտատէն ալ բերես՝ տղան քեռան կը նմանի:

9

People

"Even if you bring the bride from Baghdad, the son looks like the mother's brother."

People

1 Happy is the man, rich or poor, who finds peace in the inner sanctum of the home.

Երջանիկ է այն մարդը, ըլլայ արքայ կամ գեղջուկ, որ իր խաղաղութիւնը կը գտնէ բուն իր իսկ տան մէջ:
Yerchaneeg eh ayn martuh, uhllah arkah gam kheghjoog, vor eer haghaghootyoonuh guh kuhdneh poon eer eesg dan mech.

2 The fool said it, the wise believed it. (Naivety, trusting.)

Խենթը ըսաւ, խելօքը հաւատաց:
Khentuh uhsav, khelokuh havadats.

3 The fool dropped a rock in the well; ten wise men couldn't pull it up.

Խենթը քար մը ձգեց հորը, տասը խելօք չկրցան դուրս հանել:
Khentuh kar muh tsuhkets horuh, dasuh khelok chuhguhrtsan hanel.

4 The fool doesn't have horns. (Fools aren't obvious.)

Խենթը կոտոշով չ'ըլլար:
Khentuh godoshov chuhllar.

5 Don't laugh like crazy John. (Don't be silly. Listen. Esoteric saying.)

Խենթ Յովհաննէսին պէս մի' խնդար:
Khent Hovhannesseen bes mee khuhntar.

6 Don't send an old man for a donkey or a young man for a bride. (Be aware of foolish judgment.)

Ծեր մարդ մի' ղրկեր էշի համար, երիտասարդ մի ղրկեր հարսի համար:
Dzer mart mee ghuhrger eshee hamar, yereedasart mee ghuhrger harsee hamar.

7 Hangs a tail on everyone. (Criticism, judgment.)

Ամէն մարդու վրայ պոչ մը կը կախէ:
Amen martoo vrah boch muh guh gakheh.

8 There is no man who doesn't have a worry.

Մարդ չի կայ որ տէրտ չունի:
Mart chee gah vor derd choonee.

9 Great men make great mistakes.

Մեծ մարդիկ մեծ սխալներ կը գործեն:
Medz marteek medz skhalner guh kordzen.

10 The uncaught thief is the most honest man.

Չբռնուած գողը ամենէն ճշմարիտն է:
Chuhpuhrnuhvadz koghuh amenen juhshmareedn eh.

11 Wish well for your neighbor, so goodness will come to your head.

Բարի ուզէ դրացիիդ, որ բարի գայ գլխուդ:
Paree oozeh tuhratseeyeet, vor paree kah kuhlkhoot.

12 The thief awaits a cloudy day.

Գողը ամպոտ օրուայ կը սպասէ:
Koghuh ambod orvah guh sbaseh.

13 The thief who steals eggs will also steal chickens.

Հաւկիթին գողը հաւ ալ կը գողնայ:
Havgeeteen koghuh hav al guh koghnah.

14 Light is an enemy to the thief.

Լոյսը գողին թշնամի է:
Looysuh kogheen tuhshnameen eh.

15 Your friend looks at your head, your enemy at your feet.
(Your friend can look you in the eye, your enemy cannot.)

Բարեկամդ գլխուդ կը նայի, թշնամիդ՝ ոտքիդ:
Paregamuht kuhlkhoot guh nayee, tuhshnameet vodkeet.

16 Eat with your friend, but do not do business with him.

Բարեկամիդ հետ հա՛ց կեր, բայց առեւտուր մի՛ ըներ:
Paregameet hed hats ger, payts arevdoor mee uhner.

17 Until you eat a kilo of salt with your friend, you won't know who he is.
(Many experiences test a friend.)

Մինչեւ քիլօ մը աղ չուտես բարեկամիդ հետ, չես գիտեր թէ ով է:
Meenchev vor kilo muh agh choodes paregameet hed, ches keeder teh ov eh.

18 Have intelligent enemies, but don't have foolish friends.

Խելացի թշնամի ունեցիր, բայց խենթ բարեկամ մի՛ ունենար:
Khelatsee tuhshnamee oonetseer, payts khent paregam mee oonenar.

19 It is more acceptable to have an intelligent enemy than to have an ignorant friend.

Աւելի նախընտրելի է խելացի թշնամի ունենալ, քան թէ տգէտ բարեկամ:
Avelee nakhuhndrelee eh khelatsee tuhshnamee oonenal, kan teh duhked paregam.

20 Tell me who your friend is, and I'll tell you who you are.

Ըսէ ինծի բարեկամդ ով է, ըսեմ քեզի թէ դուն ով ես:
Uhseh eendzee paregamuht ov eh, uhsem kezee teh toon ov es.

21 All who laugh in your face are not your friends.

Ամէն երեսիդ խնդացողը բարեկամդ չէ:
Amen yereseet khuntatsoghuh paregamuht cheh.

22 A known enemy cannot be a friend to the Armenian.

Գիտցած թշնամին հայուն բարեկամ չ'ըլլար:
Keedtsadz tshnameen hayoon paregam chuhllar.

23 There is no giver of bread to the orphan, but many givers of advice.

Որբին հաց տուող չ'ըլլար, բայց խրատ տուող շատ:
Vorpeen hats duhvogh chuhllar, payts khrad duhvogh shad.

24 Don't be afraid of the obvious enemy, be afraid of the secret one.

Յայտնի թշնամիէն մի՛ վախնար, գաղտնի թշնամիէն վախցիր:
Haydnee tuhshnameeyen mee vakhnar, kaghdnee tuhshnameeyen vakhtseer.

25 The old enemy can't be a friend.

Հին թշնամին բարեկամ չ'ըլլար:
Heen tuhshnameen paregam chuhllar.

26 The Armenians are the Armenians' enemy.

Հայը հայուն թշնամին է:
Hayuh hayoon tuhshnamee eh.

27 If you give the dough to the baker, he will bake it right.
(Seek an expert.)

Հացը հացագործին եթէ տաս, շիտակ կ'եփէ:
Hatsuh hatsakordzeen yeteh das sheedag gepeh.

28 Take flour to a baker and you're still ahead, even if he takes half.
(Being cheap sometimes costs more.)

Ալիւրը հացագործին տուր, շահաւոր կ'ըլլաս, եթէ նոյնիսկ կէսը առնէ:
Alyooruh hatsakordzeen door, shahavor guhllas, yeteh nooyneesg gesuh arneh.

29 A speaker needs a listener.

Ըսողին լսող պէտք է:
Uhsogheen luhsogh bedk eh.

30 The more you call a man a fool, the more foolish he becomes.

Մարդուն որչափ յիմար ըսես, կը յիմարանայ։
Martoon vorchap heemar uhses, guh heemaranah.

31 To those who love you, be a servant; to those who don't, be a master.
(Serve those who care.)

Քեզ սիրողին ծառայ եղիր, չսիրողին աղա եղիր։
Kez seerogheen dzarah yegheer, chuhseerogheen aghah yegheer.

32 The traveler's heaviest burden is an empty wallet.

Ճամբորդին ամենածանր բեռը պարապ քսակն է։
Jamporteen amenadzanr peruh barab kuhsagn eh.

33 Half of the dwarf is above the earth, half below.
(Don't be deceived.)

Ճուճէին (կարճին) կէսը գետինին տակն է, կէսն ալ գետինին վրայ։
Joojeyeen (garjeen) gesuh kedeeneen dagn eh, gesn al kedeeneen vuhrah.

34 I'm a chief, you're a chief, who will mill the grain?

Ես աղա, դուն աղա, ջաղացքը ո՞վ աղայ։
Yes aghah toon aghah, chaghatskuh ov aghah?

35 One shame for the beggar, a double shame for the nongiver.
(A double shame for the uncharitable.)

Ուզողին մէկ ամօթ, չտուողին երկու ամօթ։
Oozogheen meg amot, chduhvogheen yergoo amot.

36 With your own belongings, you are put to shame.
(You don't get your money's worth.)

Մալովդ մալամըդ կ'ըլլաս։
Malovuht malamuht guhllas.

37 Go die, come (back), then I will love you.
(Unappreciated while alive.)

Գնա՛ մեռիր, եկուր սիրեմ։
Knah mehreer, yegoor seerem.

38 Everyone thinks his worries are as large as a camel.

Ամէն մարդ կը խորհի իր տէրտը ուղտի չափ խոշոր է։
Amen mart guh khorhee eer derduh ooghdee chap khoshor eh.

39 The fool is never unlucky, the wise man is never happy.	Ապուշը բնաւ դժբախտ չէ, խելօքը միշտ ուրախ չէ: *Abooshuh puhnav tuhzhpakhd cheh, khelokuh meeshd oorakh cheh.*
40 The poor longs for bread, the rich for everything.	Աղքատը կարօտ է հացի, հարուստը ամէն բանի: *Aghkaduh garod eh hatsee, haroosduh amen panee.*
41 Be wise, but let them think you're crazy.	Գիտնական եղիր, բայց թող խենթ կարծեն: *Keednagan yegheer, payts togh khent gardzen.*
42 They gave the beggar a cucumber. He said, "I don't want it, it's crooked."	Մուրացկանին վարունգ տուին, ըսաւ՝ չեմ ուզեր, ծուռ է: *Mooratsganeen varoonk duhveen, uhsav chem oozer, dzoor eh.*
43 False words, false money come from a false person.	Սուտ խօսքը, սուտ դրամը, սուտ մարդէն կու գայ: *Sood khoskuh, sood tuhramuh, sood marten goo kah.*
44 Our real grave is not in the ground but in the hearts of people.	Մեր իրական գերեզմանը հողին մէջ չէ, այլ մարդոց սրտին մէջ: *Mer eeragan kerezmanuh hogheen mech cheh, ayl martots seerdeen mech.*
45 Fire broke out at the liar's house, but nobody believed him.	Սուտ խօսողին տունը կրակ ինկաւ, ոչ ոք հաւատաց: *Sood khosogheen doonuh guhrag eengav, voch vok havadats.*
46 When a poor man extends his hand, it's not for greeting.	Երբ աղքատ մը ձեռքը կ'երկնցնէ, բարեւելու համար չէ: *Yerp aghkad muh tserkuh gerguhntsuhneh, pareveloo hamar cheh.*

People

47 An uninvited guest sits on thorns. (Uncomfortable, uneasy.)

Անհրաւէր հիւրը փուշի վրայ կը նստի:
Anhuhraver hyooruh pooshee vrah guh nuhsdee.

48 A lie destroys the liar's home.

Սուտը՝ սուտ ասողին տունն է քանդում:
Sooduh sood asogheen doonn eh kantoom.

49 It's hanging over my head like a Damoclean sword. (Burdened; dangerous or precarious situation.)

Դամոկլէսեան սուրին պէս գլխուս վրայ կախուած է:
Tamoglesian sooreen bes kuhlkhoos vrah gakhvadz eh.

50 He deals underhandedly.

Տակէն քալեցնող է:
Dagen kaletsuhnogh eh.

51 The world is a mill; sometimes it grinds wheat, sometimes humans.

Աշխարհը ջաղացք մըն է, երբեմն ցորեն կ'աղայ, երբեմն՝ մարդ:
Ashkharuh chaghatsk muhn eh, yerpemuhn tsorehn gaghah, yerpemuhn mart.

52 Hope is the bread of the unfortunate.

Յոյսը դժբախտներուն հացն է:
Hooysuh tuhzhpakhdneroon hatsn eh.

53 Laughter is abundant in the mouths of fools.

Խնդուքը առատ է ապուշներուն բերնին մէջ:
Khuhntookuh arad eh abooshneroon perneen mech.

54 When the peasant is poor, the country is poor.

Երբ աղքատ է գիւղացին, աղքատ է երկիրը:
Yerp aghkad eh kyooghatseen, aghkad eh yergeeruh.

55 A man's personality doesn't change until his soul leaves him.

Մինչեւ մարդուն հոգին դուրս չելլէ, բնութիւնը դուրս չ'ելլեր:
Meenchev martoon hokeen toors chelleh, puhnootyoonuh toors cheller.

56 The tailor's pocket has a hole in it.

Դերձակին գրպանը ծակ կ'ըլլայ:
Tertsageen kuhrbanuh dzag guhllah.

57 Every woman makes her own style of yogurt.

Ամէն կին իր գիտցած մածունը կը շինէ:
Amen geen eer keedtsadz madzoonuh guh sheeneh.

58 Gossip is said behind the king's back.

Թագաւորին ետեւէն խօսք կ'ըսեն:
Takavoreen yedeven khosk guhsen.

59 The fool's yarn is spun by the wind.

Խենթին մանածը հովը կը մանէ:
Khenteen manadzuh hovuh guh maneh.

60 Man with man.
(Survival means interaction.)

Մարդը մարդով է:
Martuh martov eh.

61 Give the sexton some whiskey.
(Words uttered by the priest who wants the whiskey also.)

Ժամկոչին մաստիքա մը տուր:
Zhamgocheen masdeekah muh door.

62 The fool turned the day into a day; the wise waited for the day to become a day.
(Delay makes a fool out of the intelligent one.)

Խենթը օրը օր ըրաւ, խելացին սպասեց որ օրը օր ընէ:
Khentuh oruh or uhrav, khelatseen uhsbasets vor oruh or uhllah.

63 A friend to all is a friend to none.

Ամէնուն բարեկամը ոչ մէկուն բարեկամը չէ:
Amenoon paregamuh voch megoon paregamuh cheh.

64 The fallen one has no friends.

Ինկողը բարեկամ չունի:
Eengoghuh paregam choonee.

65 Look for your enemy under your pillow.
(The enemy can come from within.)

Թշնամիդ բարձին տակը փնտռէ:
Tuhshnameet partseen daguh puhndreh.

66 Even if you know a thousand things, ask the person who knows only one.

Եթէ նոյնիսկ հազար բան գիտես, մէկ բան գիտցողին հարցուր:
Yeteh nooyneesg hazar pan keedes, meg pan keedsogheen hartsoor.

67 If you have an intelligent son, why do you need money? If you have a foolish son, why do you need money?

Եթէ խելացի տղայ ունիս, դրամը ի՞նչ ընես, եթէ խենթ տղայ ունիս, դրամը ի՞նչ ընես։
Yeteh khelatsee duhgha oonees, tuhramuh eench uhnes? Yeteh khent duhgha oonees, tuhramuh eench uhnes?

68 You don't butt your head with a fool. (Can't waste time reasoning with a fool.)

Խենթին հետ գլուխ չես դներ։
Khenteen hed kuhlookh ches tuhner.

69 Keep your door closed, so you won't catch your neighbor at thievery.

Դուռդ գոց պահէ, դրացիդ գող մի հաներ։
Tooruht kots baheh, tuhratseet kogh mee puhrner.

70 He who is content with his lot is the world's happiest man.

Ով որ իր ունեցածէն գոհ է, աշխարհին երջանիկ մարդն է։
Ov vor eer oonetsadzen koh eh, ashkhareen yerchaneeg martn eh.

71 With our money, we became fools. (We didn't get our money's worth and suffered.)

Մեր դրամով մասխարա եղանք։
Mer tuhramov maskhara yeghank.

72 By the time the intelligent one thinks it through, the fool crosses the bridge.

Մինչեւ խելացին մտածէ, խենթը կամուրջը կ'անցնի։
Meenchev khelatseen muhdadzeh, khentuh gamoorchuh gantsnee.

73 The food that comes from others is not a meal, and it's not on time.

Ուրիշէն եկածը ժում չ'ըլլար, ան ալ ժամանակին չ'ըլլար։
Ooreeshen yegadzuh zhoom chuhllar, an al zhamanageen chuhllar.

74 I wish the least of the Armenian brain belonged to me. (Turkish quote.)

Հայերուն վերջին խելքը իմս ըլլար։
Hayeroon vercheen khelkuh eemuhs uhllar.

75 It's easy to be generous with other people's money.

Դիւրին է ուրիշին դրամով առատ ըլլալ:
Tyooreen eh ooreesheen tuhramov arad uhllal.

76 Listen to elderly advice, so adversity won't touch you.

Մտիկ ըրէ մեծի խրատ, որ չիհասնի փորձանք վրադ:
Mudeeg uhreh medzee khuhrad, vor chuhasnee portsank vraht.

77 Only a handful of soil can satiate the eye of man.
(It's enough, but man wants more.)

Մարդոց աչքը միայն ափ մը հողով կը կշտանայ:
Martots achkuh meeayn ap muh hoghov guh guhshdanah.

78 The stranger's eye will not bring you light.
(Strangers are not concerned.)

Օտարին աչքը քեզի լոյս չի տար:
Odareen achkuh kezee looys chee dar.

79 If the blind leads the blind, they will both fall in the pit.

Կոյրը կոյրին եթէ առաջնորդէ, երկուքն ալ կ'իյնան փոսը:
Gooyruh gooyreen yeteh arachnorteh, yergookn al geeynan posuh.

80 In the kingdom of the blind, the one-eyed man is king.

Կոյրերու թագաւորութեան մէջ միականին թագաւոր է:
Gooyreroo takavorootyan mech meeyaganeen takavor eh.

81 Better the light go out of a man's eye than his name.

Լաւ է լոյսը մարդուն աչքէն ելլէ, քան թէ անունը:
Lav eh looysuh martoon achken yelleh, kan teh anoonuh.

82 The liar has a long tongue.
(The liar speaks many falsehoods.)

Սուտ խօսողին լեզուն երկար կ'ըլլայ:
Sood khosogheen lezoon yergar guhllah.

83 The thief's heart trembles.

Գող, սիրտը դող:
Kogh, seerduh togh.

84 Man's face is the mirror of his heart.

Դէմքը մարդուն սիրտին հայելին է:
Temkuh martoon seerdeen hayeleen eh.

85 The money of the rich is the tongue for the poor.
(The poor is the beggar.)

Հարուստին դրամը աղքատին լեզուն է:
Haroosdeen tuhramuh aghkadeen lezoon eh.

86 When you have a bad tooth, pull it out and be free. When you have a bad neighbor, pull away, move, and be free.

Գէշ ակռայ եթէ ունիս, քաշէ՛ հանէ, ազատիր: Գէշ դրացի եթէ ունիս, քաշուէ գնա՛, ազատիր:
Kesh agra yeteh oonees, kasheh haneh, azadeer. Kesh tuhratzee yeteh oonees, kashveh knah, azadeer.

87 The coward's mother doesn't cry.
(The coward doesn't enter into conflicting situations.)

Վախկոտին մայրը չի լար:
Vakhgodeen mayruh chee lar.

88 Those who have children don't need enemies.

Զաւակ ունեցողը թշնամիի պէտք չունի:
Zavag oonetsoghuh tuhshnameeyee bedk choonee.

89 The baby who doesn't cry doesn't get milk.

Չի լացող պզտիկը կաթ չունենար:
Chee latsogh buhzdeeguh gat choonenar.

90 If the child is not spanked, the knee will be slapped.
(One who doesn't spank the child will slap his own knee in regret.)

Ան որ չօճուխին չի ծեծեր ծունկին կը զարնէ:
An vor chojookheen chee dzedzer, dzoongeen guh zarneh.

91 (I) gave birth to the child, (I) didn't give birth to the nature.
(The temperament of the child is not the parent's responsibility.)

Զաւակը բերի, բնութիւնը չի բերի:
Zavaguh peree, puhnootyoonuh chee peree.

92 Don't be fooled by a woman's beauty; rather, let her character be beautiful.

Կնոջ մը գեղեցկութեան մի խաբուիր, թող բնութիւնը գեղեցիկ ըլլայ:
Guhnoch muh keghetsgootyan mee khapveer; togh puhnootyoonuh keghetseeg uhllah.

93 Before a son, now a neighbor.
(Marriage separates the bond.)

Առաջ տղաս էիր, հիմա դրացիս ես:
Arach duhghas eyeer, heemah tuhratsees ehs.

94 He hasn't had a bride, he is looking for the bride. (Confusion.)	Հարս չէ ունեցած, հարսն է կը փնտռէ: *Harss cheh oonetsadz, harssn eh guh puhndreh.*
95 Every man has a pain, every tree has a worm.	Ամէն մարդ ցաւ ունի, ամէն ծառ որդ ունի: *Amen mart tsav oonee, amen dzar vort oonee.*
96 A girl can be more worthy than seven boys.	Աղջիկ կայ որ եօթը տղայ կ'արժէ: *Aghcheeg gah vor yotuh duhghah garzheh.*
97 Man's luck doesn't change, his pillow changes. (A second marriage will not change your luck.)	Մարդուն բախտը չի փոխուիր, բարձը կը փոխուի: *Martoon pakhduh chee pokhveer, partsuh guh pokhvee.*
98 A woman who loses her husband is like a woman whose backbone is broken.	Ամուսինը կորսնցնող կին մը ողնայարը կոտրած կնոջ կը նմանի: *Amooseenuh gorsuhntsootsadz geen muh voghnaharuh godradz guhnoch guh nuhmanee.*
99 The girl who doesn't marry well lives with fantasies (wishes).	Լաւ տեղ չիյնող աղջիկը փափաքներով կ'ապրի: *Lav degh cheeynogh aghcheeguh papaknerov gabree.*
100 Everybody has a mother. (Mourning a mother is universal.)	Ամէն մարդ ալ մայր ունի: *Amen mart al mayr oonee.*
101 Man's worst enemies are a bad wife and cold weather. (Both are intolerable.)	Մարդուն ամենէն մեծ թշնամիներն են գէշ կինը եւ ցուրտ օդը: *Martoon amenen medz tuhshnameenern en kesh geenuh yev tsoord otuh.*
102 A crooked man always speaks crooked.	Սխալ մարդը միշտ սխալ կը խօսի: *Suhkhal mahrtuh meeshd suhkhal guh khossee.*
103 False friend, hidden enemy.	Սուտ բարեկամ, ներքին թշնամի: *Sood paregam, nerkeen tuhshnamee.*

People

104 From one to whom a good deed is done you will not see goodness.

Բարիք ստացող մարդէն բարիք չես տեսներ։
Pareek uhsdatsogh marten pareek ches desner.

105 If you speak to a good man, he brings goodness; if you speak to a bad man, he brings evil.

Բարի մարդոց հետ խօսիս բարիք կը բերեն, չար մարդոց հետ խօսիս չարիք կը բերեն։
Paree martots hed khosees pareek guh peren; char martots hed khosees chareek guh peren.

106 Every goodness cannot be found in one man.
(Nobody is perfect.)

Ամէն լաւութիւն մէկ մարդու վրայ չ’ըլլար։
Amen lavootyoon meg martoo vrah chuhllar.

107 There are some men who, when you spit in their face, say, "Thank God, the rain came."
(They are unaware, insensitive, shameless.)

Մարդ կայ որ եթէ երեսին վրայ թքնես, կ’ըսէ «Փառք Աստուծոյ, անձրեւ կու գայ»։
Mart gah vor yeteh yereseen vrah tuhknes, guhseh, "Park Asdoodzoh, antsrev goo kah."

108 The Lord makes the saint strong.

Տէրը սուրբը զօրաւոր կ’ընէ։
Deruh soorpuh zoravor guhneh.

109 The orphan's meal is ground by God.
(The orphan is cared for by God.)

Որբին ջաղացքը Աստուած կ’աղայ։
Vorpeen chaghatzkuh Asdvadz gagha.

110 For forty years a sinner, for one year asks forgiveness, the sin will be forgiven.
(Forgiveness is always available.)

Քառասուն տարի մեղաւորը, մէկ տարի մեղայ ըսէ, մեղքը կը ներուի։
Karasoon daree meghavoruh, meg daree meghah uhseh, meghkuh guh nervee.

111 The good I do, let God do unto my children.

Ես ընեմ, թող Աստուած ալ զաւակներուս ընէ։
Yes uhnem, togh Asdvadz al zavagneroos uhneh.

112 Fear the man who is not afraid of God or ashamed of his actions.

Աստուծմէ չվախցողէն ու մարդոցմէ չամչցողէն վախցիր։
Asdoozmeh chuhvakhtsoghen oo martotsmeh chamuhchtsoghen vakhtseer.

113 An honest man is thrown out of forty villages.

Շիտակ խօսողը քառասուն գիւղէն կը վռնտեն:
Sheedag khosogheh karasoon kyooghen guh vuhruhnden.

114 Stay away from dwarfs; God has struck them on the head.
(That's why they are short.)

Ճուճէներէն (կարճերէն) հեռու կեցիր, Աստուած իրենց գլխուն զարկած է:
Joojeneren heroo getseer, Asdvadz eerents kuhlkhoon zargadz eh.

115 God turns His face away from a shameless person.

Աստուած երեսը կը դարձնէ անամօթ մարդէն:
Asdvadz yeresuh guh tartzuhuneh anamot marten.

116 The robber from the robber stole; God saw and was amazed.

Գողը գողէն գողացաւ, Աստուած տեսաւ զարմացաւ:
Koghuh koghen koghatsav, Asdvadz desav zarmatsav.

117 The robber from the robber stole; God saw and observed with joy.

Գողը գողէն գողացաւ, Աստուած տեսաւ ուրախացաւ:
Koghuh koghen koghatsav; Asdvadz desav oorakhatsav.

118 The guest is God's messenger.
(This is said to a guest upon his arrival.)

Հիւրը Աստուածին (Աստուծոյ) պատգամաւորն է:
Hyooruh Asdvadzeen (Asdoodzo) badkamavorn eh.

119 When the rich man ate snake, they said it was medicine, but when the poor man ate it, they said he was hungry.

Հարուստը օձ կերաւ, ըսին դեղ է, իսկ երբ չունեցողը կերաւ, ըսին անօթի է:
Haroosduh ohts gerav, uhseen tegh eh, eesg yerp choonetsoghuh gerav, uhseen anotee eh.

120 One Armenian eats one chicken, two Armenians eat two chickens, three Armenians eat each other.

Մէկ հայը մէկ հաւ կ'ուտէ, երկու հայերը երկու հաւ կ'ուտեն, երեք հայերը զիրար կ'ուտեն:
Meg hayuh meg hav goodeh, yergoo hayeruh yergoo hav gooden, yerek hayeruh zeerar gooden.

121 If you tie a man and a donkey together, the donkey can't become a man, but the man can become a jackass.

Եթէ մարդն ու էշը իրարու քով կապես, էշը մարդ չի կրնար ըլլալ, բայց մարդը էշ կրնայ ըլլալ:
Yeteh martn oo eshuh eeraroo kov gabes, eshuh mart chee guhrnar uhllal, payts martuh esh guhrnah uhllal.

122 Call a man a jackass for ten days, he will become one.
(Self-fulfilling prophecy.)

Մարդը տասը օր էշ կանչես, էշ կ'ըլլայ:
Martuh dasuh or esh ganches, esh guhllah.

123 The dog doesn't recognize his master.
(Confusion.)

Շունը իր տէրը չի ճանչնար:
Shoonuh eer deruh chee janchnar.

124 The neighbor's wife looks like a bride, the neighbor's hen looks like a goose.
(Everything looks better from afar.)

Դրացիին կինը հարս կ'երեւայ, դրացիին հաւն ալ ղազ կ'երեւայ:
Tuhratseeyeen geenuh hars gerevah, tuhratseeyeen havn al ghaz gerevah.

125 The animal knows by smelling, man by talking.

Կենդանին հոտուըտալով կը գիտնայ, մարդը խօսելով:
Gentaneen hodvuhdalov guh keednah, martuh khoselov.

126 Pretending to be a fool, he ate the monastery's chickens.
(Deception; taking advantage.)

Սուտ խենթ եղած է, վանքի հաւերը կերած է:
Sood khent yeghadz eh, vankee haveruh geradzeh.

127 The orphan poured water on his head, heaven and earth darkened.
(Unfortunate.)

Որբը գլուխը ջուր դրեր է, երկինք եւ գետին մթներ են:
Vorpuh kuhlookhuh choor tuhrer eh, yergeenk yev kedeen muhtner en.

128 What can a dark-skinned person do with soap? What can a fool do with advice?

Էսմերը սապոնը ի՞նչ ընէ, խեւը խրատը ի՞նչ ընէ:
Esmeruh sabonuh eench uhneh, khevuh khuhraduh eench uhneh?

People

129 When you get old, you will understand and respect the aged.

Երբ ծերանաս, ծերին յարգը կ'իմանաս:
Yerp dzeranas, dzereen harkuh gueemanas.

130 Every man says his yogurt drink is sweet.
(Not truthful, boastful.)

Ամէն մարդ կ'ըսէ՝ թանս անուշ է:
Amen mart guhseh tahnus anoosh eh.

131 Luck and misfortune are brother and sister, they walk together.

Բախտ եւ անբախտ քոյր եղբայր են, իրարու հետ կը քալեն:
Pakhd yev anpakhd kooyr yeghpayr en, eeraroo hed guh kalen.

132 The lazy one's luck comes and settles on the knee.
(Luck falls on the lazy.)

Ծոյլին բախտը կու գայ, ծունկին վրայ կը նստի:
Dzooyleen pakhduh goo kah, dzoongeen vuhrah guh nuhsdee.

133 A righteous man may stagger, but he won't fall.

Շիտակ մարդը սերսեմլեմիշ կ'ըլլայ, բայց վար չ'իյնար:
Sheedag martuh sersemlemeesh guhllah, payts var cheeynar.

134 When anything is cheap, the customer doesn't have a conscience.
(Value is not recognized when cheap.)

Բան մը եթէ աժան է, յաճախորդը խիղճ չ'ունենար:
Pan muh yeteh azhan eh, hajakhortuh kheeghj choonenar.

135 When you see the Kurd, ask him for bread, so the Kurd won't ask you for bread.
(Preempt him.)

Քիւրտը տեսնես, հաց ուզէ, որ քիւրտը քեզմէ հաց չուզէ:
Kurduh desnes, hats oozeh, vor kurduh kezmeh hatz choozeh.

136 As many languages as you know, that's how many persons you are.

Որքան լեզու գիտես, այնքան մարդ ես:
Vorkan lezoo keedes aynkan mart es.

137 Every single tongue (language) is worthy of being one man.

Ամէն մէկ լեզու մէկ մարդ կ'արժէ:
Amen meg lezoo meg mart garzheh.

138 The sated one feeds the hungry one with small crumbs.

Կուշտը անօթիին մանր փշրեր է:
Gooshduh anoteeyeen manuhr puhshrer eh.

139 A tired man's work goes backward.

Յոգնած մարդուն գործը ետ կ'երթայ:
Hoknadz martoon kordzuh yed gertah.

140 The prophet has no respect in his hometown.

Մարգարէն իր քաղաքին մէջ յարգ չունի:
Markaren eer kaghakeen mech hark choonee.

141 They judge man from the eye of the needle.
(Extreme fault-finding.)

Ասեղին ծակէն մարդ կը դիտեն:
Asegheen dzaguen mart guh teeden.

142 The deprived one lives; woe to the depriver.

Զրկուողը ապրեր է, վա՜յ զրկողին:
Zrguhvoghuh abrer eh, vay zrgogheen.

143 The mountain can't come to the mountain, but man can come to man.
(Being helpful.)

Լեռը լերան չի հանդիպիր, մարդը մարդուն կը հանդիպի:
Leruh leran chee hanteebeer, martuh martoon guh hanteebee.

144 Armenians can squeeze water from the stone.
(Armenians are resourceful and frugal.)

Հայերը քարէն ջուր կը հանեն:
Hayeruh karen choor guh hanen.

145 The poor man went to steal, the moon came out.
(No luck.)

Աղքատը գողութեան ելաւ, լուսին ծագեցաւ:
Aghkaduh koghootyan yelav, looseen dzaketzav.

146 One who speaks in front of you will also speak behind your back.
(Gossip.)

Առջեւդ խօսողը, ետեւդ ալ կը խօսի:
Archevuht khosoghuh, yedevet al guh khossee.

147 Does the one who speaks the truth have a hole in the head?
(Being truthful brings scorn.)

Շիտակ խօսողին թէփէն ծակ կ'ըլլա՞յ:
Sheedahg khossogheen tehpehn dzahg guhllah?

148 He plays his own *duduk* (horn).
(He blows his own horn. Boasts.)

Իրեն տուտուկը կը չալէ:
Eerehn duduguh guh chahleh.

149 He is *mz mz*.
(Fussy.)

Մըզ մըզ է:
Mz mz eh.

150 He doesn't understand a word.
(Stubborn.)

Խօսք չի հասկնար:
Khosk chee hasguhnar.

151 They came here poor, and they became men; they came as men, and they became jackasses.
(They became slaves to labor.)

Խեղճ եկան հոս, մարդ եղան. մարդ եկան, էշ եղան:
Kheghj yegan hos, mart yeghan; mart yegan, esh yeghan.

152 Crude and rude.
(Coarse and unpolished.)

Կոշտ ու կոպիտ:
Goshd oo gohbeed.

153 He fights with his kaka.
(Everything is a problem for him.)

Քաքին հետ կռիւ կ'ընէ:
Kakeen hed greev guhneh.

154 The healthy one dies, the sick becomes alive.
(Life is a paradox.)

Սաղը (առողջը) կը մեռնի՝ հիւանդը կ'ողջննայ:
Saghuh (aroghchuh) guh mernee, heevantuh goghchnna.

155 Long and thin he tells a story.
(He spins a story to the last detail.)

Երկար բարակ կը պատմէ:
Yergar parag guh bahdmeh.

156 All the crazy ones have gathered around my head.
(Inundated with irrational people.)

Ամէն խենդերը իմ գլուխս ժողվեր են:
Amen khenteruh eem klookhes joghver en.

157 They have no place (for the individual).
(No respect; they shun the person.)

Բանի տեղ չեն դներ:
Panee degh chen tenehr.

158 He is looking for the donkey, while he is sitting on the donkey.
(Cannot see beyond his nose.)

Էշը կը փնտռէ, էշին վրայ նստեր է:
Eshuh guh pendreh, esheen vrah nesder eh.

159 The man is the head, the wife is the neck.
(Woman controls.)

Մարդը գլուխն է, կինը վիզն է:
Martuh klookhn eh, gueenuh veezn eh.

160 I say, I hear.
(My advice is not heeded.)

Ես կ'ըսեմ՝ ես կը լսեմ:
Yes guehssem, yes guh luhssem.

161 A man who has burned his tongue on hot milk will find himself blowing on yogurt.
(Fearful because of past experience.)

Այն մարդը որ լեզուն կ'այրէ տաք կաթէն, կը փչէ մածունին վրայ:
Ayn martuh vor lezoon gayreh dahk gahten, guh puhcheh madzooneen vra.

162 He won't be left out of anything.
(Always involved.)

Բանէ մը պակաս չի մնար:
Paneh muh bagas chee menar.

163 Mother makes bread, baby is crying.
(Mother's work is never done; multi-tasking.)

Մաման հաց, ճաղան լաց:
Maman hahts, chaghan lahts.

164 If you speak, you are bad; if you don't, you are a jackass.
(Speak the truth, and you are reviled; if you don't, you are a jackass.)

Խօսիս նէ գէշ կ'ըլլաս, չխօսիս նէ էշ կ'ըլլաս:
Khosseess ne kesh guellahs, chkhosseess ne esh guellahs.

165 Don't fall into the hands of a lawyer or a doctor.

Փաստաբան եւ բժիշկի ձեռքը չիյնաս:
Pasdapahn yev pejeeshguee tserk cheeynahs.

166 Let them explode, let their nose be mired (in mud).
(Let them be humiliated; let them suffer.)

Թող ճաթին, քիթերնին թող քսուի:
Togh jahteen, keeterneen togh kessvee.

167 Let the remaining days be yours.
(Wishing long life, usually said upon the death of a person.)

Օրերը քեզի:
Oreruh kezee.

168 I came, you went.
(I am ahead of you; it's already done.)

Ես եկայ, դուն գացիր:
Yes yega, toon kahtseer.

169 My mind flew.
(I forgot.)

Խելքս թռաւ:
Khelkuhs trahv.

170 He has no desire to be a man.
(No ambition.)

Մարդ ըլլալու փափաք չունի:
Mahrt ellaloo papahk choonee.

171 The yoke is borne from great one.
(The burden is the responsibility of the master.)

Լուծը մեծէն կը ծնի:
Loodzuh medzen guh dzenee.

172 Right now, I am fine; let God think about tomorrow.
(I leave the future to God.)

Հիմակ ու հիմա լաւ եմ: Վաղուան մասին թող Աստուած մտածէ:
Heemag oo heema lav em; vaghvahn mahsseen togh Asdvadz medadzeh.

173 *Tahp, toop.*
(Upside down, messy.)

Թափ, թուփ:
Tahp, toop.

174 He has become bigger and bigger, and yet he is small.
(Little but mature; precocious child.)

Մեծցեր-մեծցեր պզտիկցեր է:
Medztser, medztser, bezdeegtser eh.

175 He took my pity, wrapped it around my neck.
(I took on his problems.)

Խիղճս առաւ, վիզս փաթթեց:
Kheeghjuhs arav, veezuhs pattets.

176 He arranges (puts in order).
(Talks too much.)

Կը շարէ:
Guh shahreh.

177 I am a sacrifice for your soul.
(I love you.)

Հոգուդ մատաղ, քեզ ղուրպան:
Hokoot madagh, kez ghoorbahn.

178 Talk about a good man, and he appears (out of nowhere).

Լաւ մարդը իր խօսքին վրայ կու գայ:
Lahv mahrtuh eer khoskeen vra gooka.

179 He has become sixty years old, and he is just learning how to play the guitar.
(Late bloomer, too late.)

Վաթսուն տարեկան եղեր է, նոր սազ նուագել կը սորվի:
Vahtsoon daregahn yegher eh, nor sahz nvakel guh sorvee.

180 She is with liver.
(In Armenia, liver is equivalent to the heart. It means she cares for people.)

Ճիկէրով է:
Jiguerohv eh.

181 Even if you bring the bride from Baghdad, the son looks like the mother's brother.
(It doesn't matter where one is born, heredity rules.)

Հարսը Պաղտատէն ալ բերես՝ տղան քեռան կը նմանի:
Harsuh Baghdaden al peres deghahn kerahn guh nmanee.

People

182 Let him keep on barking.
(Don't pay attention.)

Թող հաչէ, հաչէ, կենայ:
Togh hacheh, hacheh guehna.

183 Let the owner enjoy the land.
(Let the owner enjoy the fruit of his labor.)

Հողը տէրը թող վայելէ:
Hoghuh dehruh togh vayeleh.

184 Let me die and end.
(Escape from hard life.)

Մեռնիմ, խալասիմ:
Merneem khalasseem.

185 Let me die and be saved.
(Escape from hard life.)

Մեռնիմ ազատիմ:
Merneem azadeem.

186 How is your present situation and your health?

Հալդ քէֆդ ինչպէ՞ս է:
Haluht, kefuht eenchbess eh?

187 Every mother-in-law must put her son-in-law on her head.
(Let every mother-in-law unconditionally support [uphold] her son-in-law.)

Ամէն զոքանչ անպայման պիտի իր փեսան գլուխին վրայ դնէ:
Amehn zokanch anbayman beedee eer pesahn klookheen verah teneh.

188 Daughter, this is the way it is: this is the Lenten month, not the month of the kaka.
(This is the sweet and happy time. Wait until the bad time comes.)

Աղջիկս, այսպէս է, ասի Պահքին ամիսն է, քաքին ամիսը չէ:
Aghcheeguhs, aysbess eh; ahssi Bahkeen ameessn eh, kahkeen ameessuh cheh.

Sources and Informants

SOURCES

There were many sources for these orally collected proverbs, and they can be organized in the following categories:

- Author's collection from childhood.
- Collected as heard.
- Informants with multiple contributions, a special group of relatives and close friends who jotted down sayings remembered and heard; they are Armaveni Adams, Sophie Jemal, Armen Mechigian, Shoushan Ozdemerci, and Susie Hoogasian Villa.
- Often-repeated popular Armenian proverbs.

INFORMANTS

Adams, Anahid Gharibian
Adams, Armaveni
Amboian, Guy
Amboyan, Jack M.
Baharozian, Irene-Ossian
Barsamian, Margaret
Bayleran, Grace
Benian, Margaret
Berberian, Ara
Boyajian, Nellie
Daghavarian, Mildred
Daghavarian, Nishan
Dakesian, Paully
Derdarian, Mae
Derderian, Almas
Doctorian, Kerop (James)
Dolik, Zaven
Garboushian, Arpeneh
Getoor, Elmon
Getoor, Dr. Levon
Gopigian, Dzaghig
Gopigian, Haig
Hanadenian, Maritza
Javizian, Alice
Jemal, Sophie
Kadian, Dr. George

Sources and Informants

Kadian, Hampartzoum
Kadian, Nevart
Kaloogian, Sarah
Kalousdian, Ardemis
Kalousdian, Diran
Karagozian, Arousiag
Kasabach, Armen
Kasabach, Arshalous
Kaye, Rose
Kazazian, Karnik
Kumjian, Nora
Laktzian, Ann
Mavian, Zorek
Mechigian, Armen
Megerian, Axelle
Megerian, Edmond
Melikshah, Hermine
Merian, Dr. Charles
Minasian, Emma
Mooradian, Ardash
Mooradian, Dickran
Mooradian, Moorad
Mooradian, Shakey
Nahabedian, Rose
Nigoghosian, Alice
Nigoghosian, Sandi
Ohanian, Krikor (actor Mike Connors)
Oknayan, Arman
Oulbegian, Hampartzoum
Oulbegian, Violet
Ozdemerci, Sahak
Ozdemerci, Shoushan
Paul, Roseanne
Raizian, Manoush
Rubyan, Reverend Puzant
Sarkesian, Horop
Sarkesian, Nevart
Sarkesian, Sepeur
Semerjian, Mida
Tazian, Sue
Telbelian, Sirvart
Terzibashian, David
Tooghigian, Lucia
Toosonian, Krikor
Tootikian, Reverend Dr. Vahan
Tootikian, Yeretzgin Rosette
Topouzian, Norma
Unknown informants
Varjabadian, Dorothy
Varjabedian, Bishop Popkin
Vart, Anahid
Vart, Dick
Villa, Susie Hoogasian
Yavruyan, Sara

Provinces, Counties, Cities, Towns, and Villages of Immigrants, Survivors, and Informants

Agin, Turkey
Aintab, Turkey
Akhalkalak, Georgia
Amasia, Turkey
Ankara, Turkey
Baku, Azerbaijan
Beirut, Lebanon
Bitlis, Turkey
Cesaria, Turkey
Devereg, Turkey
Efkerah, Turkey
Erzeroum, Turkey
Everek, Turkey
Fenesse, Turkey
Garva, Turkey
Hussenig, Turkey
Iran, various villages
Istanbul, Turkey
Jerusalem, Israel
Keghi, Turkey
Kessab, Syria
Kharpert, Turkey
Malatya, Turkey
Malmaison, France
Marseille, France
Moush, Turkey
Shabinkraissar, Turkey
Sivas, Turkey
Smyrna, Turkey
United States, various states
Van, Turkey
Yerevan, Armenia

Map of Historic Armenia

This map shows the land area of Historic Armenia as it was in about 95 BC. Countries are shown with current boundaries, and village names are shown as they were named in 1915. Names in parentheses are alternative spellings.

See *Armenia: A Historical Atlas* by Robert A. Hewsen, published by University of Chicago Press in 2000, for views of Armenia through history.

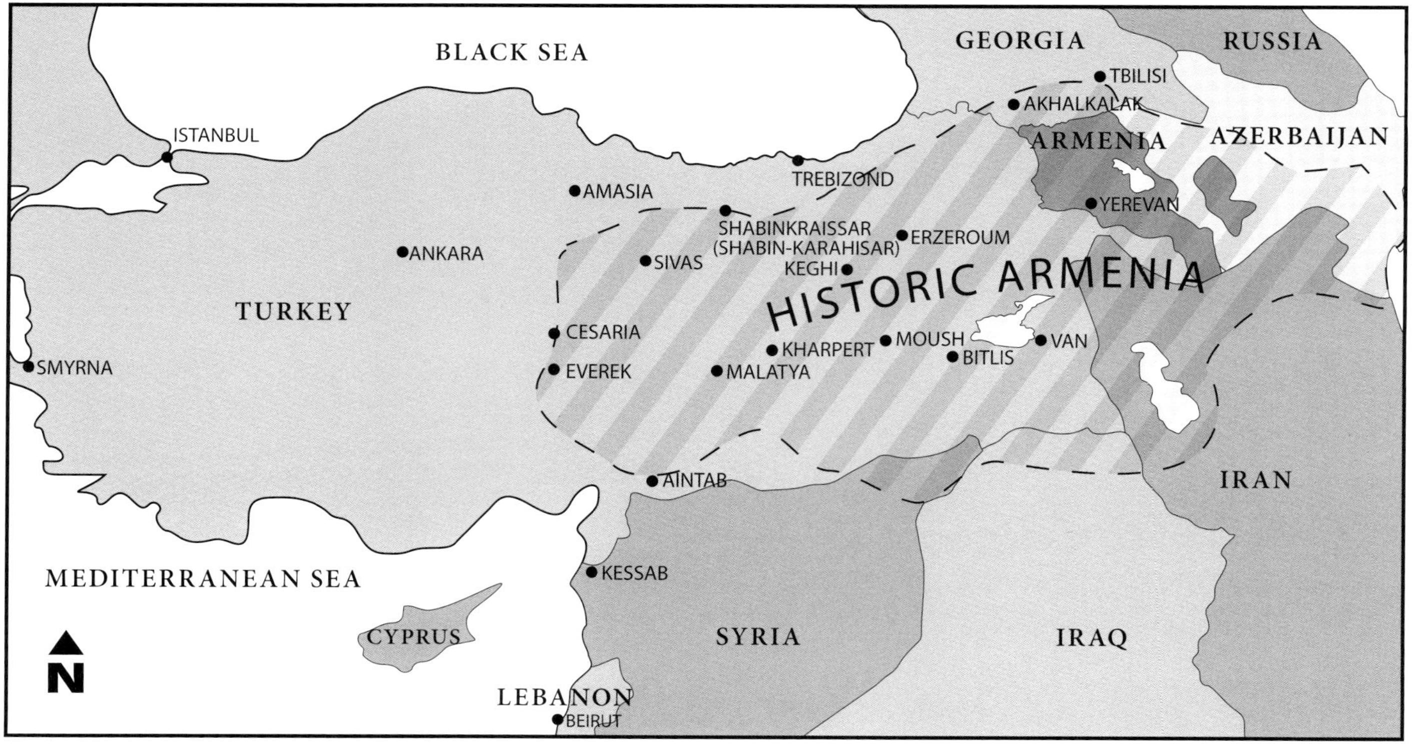

Map of Armenia

Map of the Republic of Armenia, founded May 28, 1918.

About the Author and the Illustrator

AUTHOR SUSAN KADIAN GOPIGIAN

Susan Gopigian was born in the southwest section of Detroit in the multi-ethnic community of Delray. She graduated from the University of Michigan with a liberal arts degree and received a master's degree in education from Wayne State University, followed by taking a course in folklore from Dr. James T. Callow (University of Detroit), who was instrumental in establishing the computerized format for organizing proverbs.

Gopigian taught kindergarten in Detroit Public Schools and later was a substitute teacher in the Walled Lake Consolidated School System.

For the past sixty years, she has been collecting Armenian proverbs and folklore.

She is the author of *Gadoo the Cat: An Armenian Folktale*, published in 2008 by Shoushan Books, Bloomfield Hills, MI 48301.

ILLUSTRATOR SUSAN COLLIER BOLT

Susan Bolt was born in Cleveland, Ohio. She graduated from the Cleveland Institute of Art in 1955 and took advanced studies at the Detroit Society of Creative Studies (which became the College for Creative Studies) and later at Pewabic Pottery (Michigan State University).

Bolt taught printmaking at Wayne State University and ceramics at Oak Park High School, as well as many workshops in painting, printmaking, and ceramics. She has worked professionally in the art world since 1950.

She illustrated for the *Detroit Free Press Sunday Magazine* for seven years and did free-lance illustration for the J. L. Hudson Company and Hallmark Greeting Cards. She has had several one-woman exhibitions at universities and galleries in the Midwest.

She is the illustrator of *Gadoo the Cat: An Armenian Folktale*, published in 2008 by Shoushan Books, Bloomfield Hills, MI 48301.

Susan Bolt and her husband, Russ, own and operate the Bolt Design Studio in Charlevoix, Michigan, where their children and grandchildren work to create art projects for U.S. and European clients.

The Charlevoix Circle of Arts celebrated Bolt's work in an exhibit titled "The Seasons of Sue Bolt" from August 25, 2017, through September 23, 2017.

Illustrator Susan Collier Bolt and author Susan Kadian Gopigian in Petoskey, Michigan (summer 2018).

Colophon

"A colophon is an inscription written by the scribe after he has written his manuscript, a project which could have taken years to complete. In Armenian tradition, colophons include a wealth of precious information. This is also the place where, to a certain extent, the scribe could voice his problems and complaints.

"In the colophon, the scribe must be extremely modest when writing about himself, to the point of being self-deprecating. Some colophons also included a curse to discourage people from stealing or damaging the manuscript."[1]

This modern colophon is written in the spirit and style of a medieval Armenian colophon and with only slight exaggeration.

Glory to the Most Holy Trinity of the Father and the Son and the Holy Spirit now and forever, amen. This book of proverbs was published in the year of the Armenian era 1468, in the year of our Lord 2019, after being written during many decades in Harbor Springs and Bloomfield Hills, in the State of Michigan.

Here I am Susan, also known as Shoushanig, a doddering octogenarian, priming an aged cerebellum to put a story into a book. These thoughts and memories have floated in my mind aimlessly. I lack the agility to grasp all of them but caught a few to complete my humble experience of bygone childhood years in Delray to present to you, my audience. The lucidity of my childhood looms up mightily as I look back, while the "now years" have lost luminosity.

Since I've lived longer than deemed possible, some facts and memories have been overshadowed by the exigencies of life, but I have forged onward with this aging brain to write of the reaped harvest of Armenian folklore, or it would be lost for our progeny.

With humility, I beg your patience and forbearance if this writing seems fantasized. My half-witted memory and work have been written and rewritten more than twenty-two times, aided with changes from editors and readers. I have been plagued with the arduous task of translating and transliterating the many proverbs

---

1 Sylvie Merian, ed., *A Legacy of Armenian Treasures–Testimony to a People: The Alex and Marie Manoogian Museum* (Taylor, Mich.: Alex and Marie Manoogian Foundation, 2013; distributed by Indiana University Press), p. 336.

and stymied by the vernacular of the Armenian language as heard from Istanbul to Van. After decades of wearisome travail, graciously, God has allowed this labor to come to fruition. Cleverly, He has erased the inane and nonsensical verbiage so that you, the reader, can realize a past time of the immigrants' life in America.

Accept with kindness this heartfelt manuscript, and close one eye to misprints and errors, and cover one ear if criticism daunts the spirit in which it was written. Curse those who change or otherwise minimalize the importance of this text or who would deny the suffering of my people and rewrite their history. A blessing on those who keep oral tradition alive to perpetuate our Armenian heritage.

And please, oh, readers of this colophon, remember in your heavenward prayers my beloved husband, Hachig, who was transferred to Christ before the writing of this book was finished.

Upon completion of this proverb collection comes joy with wisdom. Let's dwell on this and praise God for His tender mercies. *Der voghormya, Der voghormya, Der voghormya* (Lord have mercy, Lord have mercy, Lord have mercy). Amen and amen.